P9-DBJ-130

THE GREAT BOOK OF IRELAND

Interesting Stories, Irish
History & Random Facts
About Ireland

History & Fun Facts

BILL O'NEILL

ISBN: 9781798649596

Copyright © 2019 by LAK Publishing

ALL RIGHTS RESERVED

No part of this book may be reproduced, stored in a retrieval system, or transmitted in any form or by any means, electronic, mechanical, photocopying, recording, scanning, or otherwise, without the prior written permission of the publisher.

DON'T FORGET YOUR FREE BOOKS

GET THEM FOR FREE ON
WWW.TRIVIABILL.COM

CHAPTER THREE
ST. PATRICK'S DAY, LEPRECHAUNS, AND
MORE! 55

Leprechauns Have No Actual Connection to St.

CHAPTER FIVE

CHAPTER SIX
WEIRD IRELAND: FOLKLORE, UNSOLVED MYSTERIES, AND MORE!

INTRODUCTION

What do you know about Ireland?

Sure, you know about leprechauns. You know that you're supposed to wear green on St. Patrick's Day. But do you know where the phrase "Kiss me, I'm Irish" came from? Do you know what leprechauns have to do with St. Patrick's Day?

What do you know about St. Patrick himself? Do you know if he was even really a Saint?

You know that Ireland is full of greenery, but do you know how the country gained its nickname "The Emerald Isle"?

Do you know who gave the city of Dublin its name and why?

Do you know which American holiday got its origins from Ireland? Hint: I'm not talking about St. Patrick's Day.

Do you know which products, foods or inventions came from Ireland?

If you have ever wondered about the answers to these or other questions about Ireland, then you've come to the right place. This isn't just any book about Ireland. It's filled with interesting facts and stories about the Emerald Isle. Whether you live in Ireland or you're thinking of taking a trip there, you're bound to learn something new about the country. Once you've finished reading, you'll know so much about Ireland that you'll even impress your friends on trivia night!

Ireland is a country that's rich in both history and culture. We'll bounce around some as we look at some of the most interesting historical facts about the Emerald Isle. You'll learn more about Ireland's pop culture, attractions, folklore, and so much more!

This book is broken up into six easy to follow chapters that will help you learn more about Ireland. Then we'll find out how much attention you've been paying with trivia questions at the end of each chapter.

Some of the facts you'll read about are surprising. Some of them are weird. Some of them are cool. One thing they have in common is that they're all interesting! Once you've finished reading this book, you'll be guaranteed to walk away with more than you ever wanted to know about the Emerald Isle.

This book will answer the following questions:

How did Ireland get its name?

Why is it known as the Emerald Isle?

Who was St. Patrick really?

What do leprechauns and shamrocks have to do with St. Patrick's Day?

Which famous English game actually started out in Ireland?

How was Bailey's Irish Cream invented?

Which Irish company had a 9,000-year lease?

What is Ireland's top attraction?

Which movies have been filmed in Ireland?

Which famous novel may have been based on an Irish myth?

Which legends did the Irish believe in?

And so much more!

CHAPTER ONE

IRELAND'S HISTORY AND OTHER FACTS

Ireland, which is located in the Atlantic Ocean, is a part of the British Isles. The Irish Sea separates the country from Great Britain. How much do you really know about the country? Do you know how Ireland got its name? Do you know why its nickname is the Emerald Isle? Do you know which American holiday originated from Ireland? Hint: I'm *not* talking about St. Patrick's Day! Read on to find out the answers to these and other interesting facts about Ireland's history!

How Ireland Got Its Name

Have you ever wondered where Ireland's name came from?

The history of the country's name is long and drawn out. For starters, you should know that the country wasn't always known as "Ireland."

It's believed that Ireland was first known as "Inis na

Fidbadh," which means "Isle of the Woods." The name was given to the country by the Vikings, who were the first to stumble on the island. They also might have originally referred to Ireland as the "westland isle."

It was also believed that the earliest Celts may have originally referred to Ireland as the "Abundant Land." The Greeks and Romans, however, called the island "Hibernia," which translates to "land of winter." The name "Hibernia" is still frequently used by organizations and companies throughout Ireland today.

It's thought that the word Ireland originated from the old Irish word Éire," which stems from Ériu, who was a Gaelic goddess. According to Irish mythology, Ériu was believed to be the Goddess of the island, as well as the Goddess of sovereignty. The Germanic word "land" was added to the end of "Ire" to make up "Ireland."

Given the strong pagan beliefs that have historically run rampant through Ireland, this theory seems extremely likely.

Ireland's Capital Was Named by Vikings, Who Once Ruled Over the Land

Dublin is the capital of Ireland. It might surprise you to learn that the city wasn't named by the Irish but instead by the Vikings.

During the 8th and 9th centuries, the Vikings raided Ireland. They established a settlement, which they called Dubh Linn, which translate to "black pool." They named the settlement after the lake where they anchored their boats. They also referred to their settlement as the "Norse Kingdom of Dublin."

It might surprise you to learn that the Vikings also ruled over Dublin for nearly 700 years. Their rule came to an end in 1169 when the Mac Murrough, King of Leinster, asked for the help of Strongbow, the Earl of Pembroke, to conquer Dublin. After the King's death, Strongbow declared himself the King of Leinster. He then went on to defeat both the Vikings and the High King of Ireland.

However, Strongbow's rule over Ireland didn't last long. The King of England feared that Strongbow would become too powerful. The King of England declared himself Lord of Ireland. As a result, Dublin was given to the merchants of Bristol, England.

Why Ireland is Called the Emerald Isle

Ireland's nickname, the Emerald Isle, might lead you to think that the gemstone is mined in the state. Sorry to be the bearer of bad news, but there are no emerald mines in Ireland. So, how did the country get its name?

Ireland's greenery plays a huge role in why it's been dubbed the Emerald Isle. If you have ever flown above the country, then its nickname will make perfect sense. But, ultimately, we can thank poet William Drennan for the nickname.

Drennan was the first to ever refer to Ireland as "the Emerald Isle" in his 1795 poem, which was titled *When Erin First Rose*. It's unknown if someone else might have originally coined the term, but Drennan was the first one to have ever used it in print, so he's generally credited with giving Ireland its famous nickname.

Ireland is Divided into Two Parts

You may already know that Ireland is divided into Northern Ireland and the Republic of Ireland. Have you ever wondered why this is?

The split occurred during the Partition in 1921. Formally known as the Government of Ireland Act 1920, the partition was designed to create two self-governing territories in Ireland. Both of the territories were intended to remain within the United Kingdom. The Act of 1920 had provisions that would eventually reunite the two territories.

The Easter Rising also played a key role in the divide. The Easter Rising, which is also commonly referred to as the Uprising of 1916 or the Easter Rebellion, is one of the most significant events to have ever taken place in the history of Ireland.

On Easter Week in April of 1916, the Rising was started by Republicans in Ireland who wanted to end British rule in the country. Their goal was to form an independent Irish Republic. They thought it was a good time to rise against the United Kingdom, since it was already very much engaged in World War I.

The Uprising of 1916 lasted for six days, beginning on Easter Monday. It was led by Patrick Pearse, who was a schoolmaster and Irish language activist. He was joined by James Connolly's smaller Irish Citizen Army, as well as 200 women. They seized locations throughout Dublin and proclaimed an Irish Republic.

The British Army brought in thousands of reinforcements. In addition to having higher numbers, the British Army also had heavier weapons. They were able to stop the Rising. They also made approximately 3,500 Irish people prisoners, many who had no role in the Rising. About half of those were sent to internment camps or prisons in Britain.

The Easter Rising ultimately led to the Irish War of Independence. The war was fought between the years of 1919 and 1921. The war resulted in the Anglo-Irish Treaty. The treaty allowed the southern part of Ireland to become a free state. It called itself the Republic of Ireland. The treaty said that Northern Ireland could opt out of the Irish free state, which it did. Northern Ireland remained a part of the United Kingdom, which it is to this day. The Republic of

Ireland, which is often just referred to as "Ireland," remains independent to this day.

Northern Ireland and the Republic of Ireland are considered to be the same country. The two are considered different territories or states, however.

There has been talk over the years of Northern Ireland and the Republic of Ireland reuniting again to form one country again. However, it doesn't appear that this will be happening anytime soon... if ever.

Ireland Continued to Export Food to This Country During the Irish Potato Famine

Chances are, you've probably heard of the Irish Potato Famine. But did you know that Ireland continued to export food, mostly to Great Britain, during this historical tragedy that caused many of the country's citizens to starve to death?

Also referred to as the Great Hunger, the Irish Potato Famine started in 1845 as a result of a fungus-like organism called *Phytophthora infestan*s that destroyed approximately half of the country's potato crop. Over the course of the next seven years, 75% of the country's crop was destroyed as a result of *P. infestans.*

Since Ireland's farmers relied heavily on potatoes as a source of food, the destruction of the crops left many without food. By 1852, the potato crops had fully recovered. But by that time, the Potato Famine had already caused nearly one million Irish to die from starvation or issues related to malnutrition. Another million people were forced to leave Ireland as refugees.

It might surprise you to learn that Ireland continued to export food, mainly to Great Britain, during this tragic time. In fact, not only did Ireland continue to export large amounts of food to Great Britain, but researchers have found that the exportation of livestock and butter increased during the Potato Famine. Historical records suggest that rabbits, fish, honey, peas, and beans were all exported from the country, even though the Great Hunger caused so many deaths among Ireland's own population.

Ireland Was Home to This Legendary Pirate Queen

Today, she's one of the most famous pirates of all-time. While she exists in folklore, she was a real historical figure. Some might compare her to the female version of Black Beard—and she's from the Emerald Isle! Based on her name, you may have already guessed that legendary "Pirate Queen" Grace O'Malley was from Ireland.

Born in Ireland around 1530, Grace O'Malley was the daughter of Owen O'Malley, a wealthy sea trader. When Owen O'Malley died, Grace inherited his shipping and trading business.

Grace O'Malley rejected the role of a 16th century woman. Instead, she opted for a life on the sea with the fleet of her trading ships. Between the income from her business and land that she inherited from her mother, O'Malley possessed both wealth and power.

O'Malley commanded hundreds of men, along with 20 ships. They raided rival clans and merchant ships. Government officials repeatedly tried to stop her activity.

The O'Malley's were one of only a few seafaring families who lived on Ireland's west coast. Their territory was surrounded by castles for protection. They had a base at Rockfleet Castle, where they allegedly attacked ships. They also ransacked from Scotland's outlying islands and charged taxes to those who fishers off their coasts. O'Malley's ships would stop traders and demand money or a portion of their cargo if they wanted to access the rest of the Galway. Those who didn't pay the toll were attacked or murdered.

In 1574, English forces sieged Grace O'Malley Rockfleet Castle. However, O'Malley's forces attacked back, forcing the English to quickly retreat.

When she was 56 years old, O'Malley was captured by Sir Richard Bingham, a governor who the English had appointed to rule over Irish territories. O'Malley narrowly escaped a death sentence.

Eventually, O'Malley lost her land and her influence and, over time, her wealth dwindled until she was she was on the brink of poverty. When she learned that her brother and son had been captured by the English, O'Malley went to England where she met with Queen Elizabeth I. Grace O'Malley convinced the Queen to not only free her family but also to restore her lands.

Grace O'Malley died at Rockfleet Castle in 1603.

The Irish Flag's Colors Have Meanings

Did you know that the Irish flag colors have a meaning? The colors of the flag are green, white, and orange.

Here's what the colors mean:

- Green: This color represents the Gaelic Irish tradition in Ireland.
- Orange: This color represents the Protestant tradition in Ireland.
- White: This color, which is located in between the green and orange on the flag, represents a place where the Gaelic Irish and the Protestants can harmonize.

The flag was designed by Thomas Francis Meagher in 1848. Inspired by the French flag, the Irish flag wasn't raised in Dublin until after the rising in 1916.

Ireland's National Symbol is Not a Shamrock

Do you know what the national symbol of Ireland is? Thanks to St. Patrick's Day and leprechauns, you might guess that shamrocks are the country's symbol. It might come as a surprise to learn that Ireland's national symbol is *not* a shamrock!

So, what *is* Ireland's national symbol? The Harp! Interestingly, Ireland is the only country in the entire world that has a musical instrument as its national symbol.

Some of the oldest harps in the world can be found at Trinity College in Dublin. The university houses the oldest harp in Ireland, which is believed to date back to the 15th century. Constructed of oak and willow, the 29-stringed instrument was used as the model for the symbol of Ireland.

This American Holiday Originated from Ireland

Today, it's one of the most commercial holidays in the United States, with 25% of all American candy being purchased for this day. Did you know that Halloween originated from Ireland?

Halloween originates from Samhain, a Gaelic harvest festival that's held on October 31st. The festival signifies the end of summer and the beginning of winter or the "darker half" of the year.

Traditionally, the Celtics believed that Samhain was a time when our world and the spirit world are most connected. They celebrated on the day that they believed the ghosts of the dead were able to return to earth.

On Samhain, the Celts built fires where they burnt crops and animals in a sacrificial ritual to the deities. The Celts also wore costumes, which they made from animal heads and skin. They also told one another's fortunes.

When Christian influence began to spread through former Celtic lands, they renamed Samhain "All Hallows Eve," with November 1st being "All Souls Day." It was celebrated in a similar fashion to Samhain. People took part in parades and held big bonfires. They also dressed up in costumes and saints, angels, and devils. Over time, "All Hallows Eve" became known as Halloween.

It was the Irish who brought Halloween to America. The millions of Irish people who fled to America during the Potato Famine helped to popularize the holiday. Even so, early on, it was rare for celebrations of Halloween to take place in early Colonial America, due to the strong Protestant beliefs. It was first celebrated in the southernmost states, as well as Maryland.

Although the American version of the holiday has evolved over time, some things still remain the same.

People continue to wear costumes in celebration of the holiday, and many Americans believe that Halloween is the one day of the year when spirits can cross over into our realm. During the 1800s, young American women celebrating the holiday believed that yarn, mirror or apple tricks could help them uncover the name of their future husband, which is a fun pastime for many young American girls today and stems from those fortune readings back at the Samhain festivals in Ireland!

The Titanic Was Built in Ireland

If you ever saw the movie *Titanic*, starring Leonardo DiCaprio and Kate Winslet, then you may remember that the famous ship was built in Ireland.

The *RMS Titanic* was constructed by 15,000 Irishmen at the Harland and Wolff shipyard in Northern Island's capital city, Belfast. Before it made its famous voyage from Northampton in England, the Titanic was docked in Cobh, County Cork.

When the Titanic sunk on April 15th, 1912, approximately 1,503 lives were lost. The tragedy was a huge blow to the city's pride. It was in Belfast that the ship was first declared "seaworthy." While so many lives were lost when the ship hit an iceberg because they weren't enough lifeboats for all of the ship's passengers, many questioned how skilled the Irish who built the ship were.

In addition to being constructed in Ireland, the ship also carried hundreds of Irish people who set out for America in hopes of starting a new life when it sailed back in 1912.

The White House Was Built by an Irishman

Did you know America's White House was built by an Irishman?

Back in 1792, George Washington and Thomas Jefferson held a competition to decide who would build the official residence and workplace of the President of the United States.

The winner of the competition was James Hoban. Hoban was born in Ireland, where he studied architectures. He had also built the Charleston County Courthouse, which George Washington saw and liked. Washington invited Hoban to enter the competition for the White House design. His submission was chosen.

It might surprise you to learn that not only did James Hoban design and build the White House, but he did it *twice!* When the White House was destroyed by British troops during the War of 1812, Hoban redesigned and rebuilt it.

Ireland Was One of the First Countries to Use This

In 1999, Ireland became one of the first European Union nations to start using the euro. Ireland also has its own version of the 1-euro coin, which has the country's symbol—the harp—displayed on it.

Although the euro has played a key role in unifying Europe, it hasn't been without its problems. Just like Greece and Portugal, Ireland fell on hard times. With new austerity measures, such as raising taxes and cutting spending, put in place in 2008, Ireland's economy has been improving.

St. Valentine's Ashes are Buried in Ireland

Did you know that St. Valentine's ashes are buried in the Emerald Isle?

Mostly associated with the tradition of courtly love and, of course, Valentine's Day, St. Valentine wasn't from Ireland. He lived in Rome during the 3rd century.

St. Valentine's ashes were brought to Ireland from Rome by an Irish Carmelite, who had been given the ashes as a gift from Pope Gregory XVI. Another one of the Pope's gifts was a small vessel, which had been tinged with St. Valentine's blood.

The ashes are buried in a shrine, which is located inside Whitefriar Street Church in Dublin, Ireland.

The shrine is frequently visited by couples who ask St. Valentine to help bless them with long, happy lives together.

Sports Are Really Popular in Ireland

Like many other countries, sports are very popular in the Emerald Isle. Have you ever wondered what the most popular sports in Ireland are? They are as follows:

- Rugby: Recognized as the most popular sport in the country, the Irish are known to be extremely passionate about the sport. In fact, the Irish ranked 2nd in the world with their international rugby squad.
- Gaelic Football: Considered to be another one of the most popular sports in Ireland, Gaelic football differs from American football because players use both their hands *and* feet to get the ball in the back of the net or over the bar (which acts as the field goal in American football). The Gaelic Games, which is made up of both Gaelic football and hurling, is the country's national sport.
- Gaelic Hurling: Almost as popular as Gaelic football, Gaelic hurling is much like Gaelic football. However, the ball is closer to the size of a tennis ball and players used hooked shape sticks known as hurleys to hit the ball.

- Golf: Golf is considered to be one of Ireland's most successful sports. The country has produced elite players, including Rory McElroy and Graeme McDowell. America's Tiger Woods has even expressed how much he loves the golf courses in the Emerald Isle. Royal Portrush Golf Club in Northern Ireland is recognized as one of the finest courses in the world.
- Horseracing: The Celts had a deep love of horses, so it's no surprise that horseracing is one of the country's most beloved sports. Like golf, horseracing has produced some of the most famed jockeys in the world. These include AP McCoy and Ruby Walsh. There are annual races at Galway, Punchestown, and Leopardstown. Just like in America, there are betting shops for horseraces.
- Soccer: While it's not the most popular sport in Ireland, it's still a beloved sport in the country. Soccer in Ireland is split into two branches: The Republic of Ireland and Northern Ireland.

Ireland's most popular sports game is the All-Irish National, which consists of Gaelic Football and Hurling. It's held each year at Croke Park in Dublin, which is the largest sports stadium in Ireland and the 4th largest sports stadium in all of Europe.

Legend Has It That the Irish May Have Found America First

Did you know that the Irish may have been the first to discover America?

Although Christopher Columbus is credited as being with the first explorer to discover America, there have been other theories on who really found the country first. Some say the Vikings were the first to stumble on the country, while others believe the Chinese were the first to find it.

However, there's an old legend that says that an Irish monk named St. Brendan and his crew of monks may have been the first to discover America. According to the legend, St. Brendan set out to find paradise. After seven years, he came across an island that was so big that even after 40 days, he and his fellow monks were unable to reach the far shore.

This expedition is said to have taken place in the 6th century—long before Christopher Columbus ever stumbled on America in 1492! That being said, no one has ever been able to prove or disprove this theory.

RANDOM FACTS

1. Ireland is the 2nd largest island in the British Isles and the 3rd largest island in Europe, but don't let that fool you. Ireland is actually a very small country. It's 32,595 square miles—just a bit larger than the state of Maryland, which is 32,133 square miles. Ireland is only 300 miles at its longest point and 190 miles at its widest point. The United States is approximately 140 times larger than the Emerald Isle, while Russia is 202 times the size of Ireland! The country is so small that Facebook allegedly gives Ireland's residents celebrities as suggestions for its "People You May Know" feature.

2. As of 2018, Ireland was estimated to have a population of approximately 4.8 million people. For comparison's sake, the United States has a population of 326 million—meaning there are about 67 Americans for every Irish person. The United States population didn't always outnumber Ireland's population, however. Back in the year 1800, the Irish population was twice the size of America's population.

3. More Irish people live in other countries than they do in Ireland. There are more than 34

million Americans who are believed to have Irish ancestry — which is more than seven times Ireland's population of approximately 4.8 million! It's been estimated that nearly one out of every two Australians are also part Irish. Studies have also found that nearly 80 million people throughout the world also have Irish passports.

4. Ireland is made up of both provinces and counties. The provinces existed prior to the divide between the Republic of Ireland and Northern Ireland. They are still thought of as provinces that exist today, though they have no legal status in the country. The four provinces in Ireland and their main cities are Leinster (Dublin), Munster (Cork), Connacht (Galway), and Ulster (Belfast). Ireland is also made up of 32 counties: County Antrim, County Armagh, County Cavan, County Carlow, County Clare, County Cork, County Derry (or, formally, Londonderry), County Donegal, County Down, County Dublin, County Fermanagh, County Galway, County Kerry, County Kildare, County Kilkenny, County Laois, County Leitrim, County Limerick, County Longford, County Louth, County Mayo, County Meath, County Monaghan, County Offaly, County Roscommon, County Sligo, County Tipperary, County Tyrone, County Waterford, County Westmeath, County Wexford, and County

Wicklow. The largest county is County Cork, while the smallest is County Louth. County Tyrone is the largest county in Northern Ireland.

5. Although the majority of the country is rural, most of Ireland's population lives near Dublin. In fact, more than 25% of the country's population lives in or near Dublin. It's estimated that of Ireland's population of approximately 4.7 million, about 1.8 million live in Dublin. Galway and Kilkenny are also large cities in Ireland, but most of the country's rural areas have a low population density.

6. Dublin is home to many young people. In fact, estimates have found that nearly one out of every two people who live in the city is under the age of 25. This makes Dublin the European city with the youngest population. Speaking of age, the drinking age in Ireland is only 18.

7. Pub culture is very popular in the Emerald Isle. Pubs are a place for people to gather socially and form social identities. Live entertainment in the form of singing and playing music and drinking ale are commonplace in pubs. There are 666 licensed pubs in Dublin. There has been a long debate over which of Dublin's pubs is the oldest. The Brazen Head is the oldest pub in the city, dating back to its establishment as a coach house in 1198 AD. Meanwhile, Liscannor in Clare

County has the highest pub to person ratio, with one pub for approximately every 26 people.

8. A common stereotype is that Irish people are the biggest drinkers of alcohol in the world. This is a myth. Ireland is not the top country for alcohol consumption, but according to 2018 reports, it is ranked high on the list. According to the *Irish Mirror*, Ireland ranks at No. 4 with the 123 liters of alcohol each of its residents drank on average in 2017. The top country for alcohol consumption was the Czech Republic, followed by Germany and Austria. While Ireland doesn't rank highest for alcohol consumption, they *do* rank at No. 1 in terms of tea consumption! On average, every person in Ireland consumes 1,184 cups of tea per year.

9. Ireland is a very religious country. More than 85% of Ireland's citizens are Roman Catholic. The Republic of Ireland has one of the highest rates of Roman Catholic church attendance in the Western World, with about 45% regularly attending Mass. Only 10% of the Irish population identifies as not having a religious affiliation. This is in comparison to the United States, which is estimated to have a population of about 22.8% not having a religious affiliation.

10. A lot of Irish names begin with "Mac" (or "Mc") or "O'." "Mac/Mc" means "son of …", while "O"

means "grandson of …" in the Gaelic language. So, for example, the name "O'Brien" would translate to "the grandson of Brien." Over time, of course, these names come to mean "descendant of…". The name "MacAllen" would translate to "the son of Allen." So, why don't all people with Irish ancestry have a name that starts with "Mac/Mc" or "O'"? These types of names were only given to Ireland's most noble people. At one point in time, the "Allen" or the "Brien" in any given name was considered noble enough to earn a surname that his ancestors would have been proud to have. It was common for Irish people to have occupational surnames, which told what a person's family did for a living. Some examples of these types of last names include Cooper, Mason, Butler, Fisher, Archer, and Cook. Some Irish surnames that once began with O' have also been shortened over time. An example of this is Gallagher, which was once was and, in some instances, still may be, O'Gallagher. The meaning of this popular Irish surname is "descendant of Gallchobhar".

11. While English is the main language that is spoken in Ireland, some people still speak the country's ancestral language, Irish Gaelic. (When people call it the "Irish" language, they are referring to Irish Gaelic). Historically, Gaelic was

the language spoken in Ireland until it was forbidden by the British Empire during the 17th century. That being said, more people in Ireland speak Polish than they do Gaelic. Estimates have found that there are 119,526 Polish speakers and only 82,600 Gaelic speakers living in Ireland. This means that only about 2% of Ireland's population speaks Gaelic.

12. Ireland's first female president was elected in 1990. Mary Robinson was a woman who had socialist and feminist views. Her election marked liberalism in Ireland, which had been a very conservative country prior to that.

13. A popular stereotype is that all or most Irish people have bright red hair. This is another one of the myths about the Irish. Only about 9% of people in the country have red hair. That being said, it's been estimated that nearly half of Irish people carry the redheaded gene, even though they do not have red hair themselves.

14. Like most countries throughout the world, Ireland has a number of strange laws. It's illegal to wrestle tigers and hug bears (which was legal up until 1897 when many performers took part in these dangerous practices). It's technically illegal to go to the cinema on a Sunday in Northern Ireland. It's illegal to receive free alcohol.

15. Ireland is the largest exporter of software in the entire world! Google, Apple, IBM, Microsoft, Dell, Intel, and Motorola are a few of the many software companies that have headquarters in Ireland. As of 2015, one out of four of Europe's computers is made in Ireland.

16. An unusual Irish birthday tradition is to lift the birthday child upside down and gently bump his or her head against the ground for good luck. The number of times the child's head will be bumped against the ground should be his or her age, plus one.

17. Legend has it that the word "quiz" originated from Ireland. It has been said that Richard Daly, who owned a theatre in Dublin, made a bet that he could invent a word and make it so that the people throughout the city would know it in days. He allegedly had his employees write it all over the walls and it was known within days. Some historians argue that this is really nothing more than a legend and that quiz was already used in other places at the time…

18. All polar bears that are alive today originated from one Irish female brown bear. It was once believed that polar bears could trace their origins to the brown bears that lived off the coast of Alaska. In 2011, results from a DNA were released that confirmed that all of the world's

polar bears could be traced back to Irish brown bears. It's believed that the bears split into separate species between 400,000 and 2 million years ago. Irish brown bears are extinct today. The teeth and skeletons of 17 brown bears that had been discovered near caves throughout Ireland were used to determine these results.

19. Lambay Island, which is an island off the coast of Dublin, is home to a small population of red-necked wallabies. The wallabies were brought to the island by Rupert Baring during the 1950s. The Dublin Zoo also rehomed some of the wallabies it was unable to care for at the island during the 1980s. As of 2017, it was estimated that there were approximately 100 wallabies on the island. The island is also home to the only colony of grey seals on Ireland's east coast.

20. Ireland became the first European country to announce that its waters were a sanctuary for whales and dolphins. Since the decision was made in 1991, the country has seen a major increase in whale-watching, which is mostly done on Ireland's southwest coast. Fin whales (which are the 2nd largest whale in the world), Humpback whales, and dolphins are all commonly observed in the country. Rockabill and Lamaby islands are said to be some of the best places in Ireland to see harbor porpoises.

Test Yourself – Questions

1. Dublin has which of the following meanings?

    a. Black swamp
    b. Black pool
    c. Black river

2. Which American holiday originated from Ireland?

    a. Easter
    b. Halloween
    c. Christmas

3. Ireland divided into the Republic of Ireland and Northern Ireland in:

    a. 1999
    b. 1820
    c. 1921

4. Ireland ranks No. 1 for consumption of which of the following beverages?

    a. tea
    b. beer
    c. coffee

5. The Titanic was built in which of Ireland's cities?

    a. Belfast
    b. Dublin
    c. Galway

Answers

1. b.

2. b.

3. c.

4. a.

5. a.

CHAPTER TWO

IRELAND'S POP CULTURE

How much do you know about Ireland's pop culture? Do you know which movies and shows have been filmed in the country? Do you know which celebrities who are recognized throughout the world are from Ireland? Do you know which 90s boy bands are from the country or which member from a more recent boy band is from the Emerald Isle? Do you know which of Ireland's most famous tourist attractions has been featured in several movies and music videos? Do you know which famous writers are from the Emerald Isle? To learn more about Ireland's pop culture, read on!

The Movie *Tristan and Isolde* is Based on a Celtic Legend

Thanks to the 2006 film *Tristan and Isolde*, you've probably heard of the couple, who is most often compared to Romeo and Juliet. But did you know that the story of Tristan and Isolde is based on an old Celtic legend from the 12th century?

(Spoiler Alert). Although it has been retold in many forms, the legend goes like this:

Irish princess Isolde was engaged to King Mark of Cornwall, but she fell in love with his nephew, Tristan. Tristan was a knight.

The two of them ran away together, even though they were star-crossed lovers.

Tristan is eventually poisoned. After his death, Isolde dies of a broken heart. The two were allegedly buried side by side. A pair of hazel and honeysuckles is said to have grown, intertwined, from their graves.

Today, the village of Chapelizod is named after the chapel of Isolde. This is where Tristan allegedly asked Isolde to marry him.

The tale of Tristan and Isolde is considered to be one of the most influential love stories of the medieval period.

So, is the tale true? No one knows for sure and it's mostly regarded as fiction, but there has been some speculation that the real Tristan may have been the Pictish prince, whose name was Drust. He was Talorc's son. He allegedly lived in the Highlands, Scotland in the year of 780. Drust allegedly saved a princess from pirates. In later tales of this story, Drust's name evolved to Drystan, who was the King's nephew and had an affair with his wife. It's possible that, over time, the story evolved into the tale of Tristan and Isolde.

The Band U2 is From Ireland

Did you know the band U2 is from Ireland? The rock band was formed in Dublin back in 1976. The most well-known member of the band is lead vocalist and Dublin native Bono. Other members of the band include the Edge, Adam Clayton, and Larry Mullen Jr.

Well-known for their elaborate tours, U2 was formed when the members were teenagers. They were attending Mount Temple Comprehensive School in Clontarf, Dublin. Four years after their formation, the band signed with Island Records, a Jamaican-British record label. Their first album, which was titled *Boy*, was released in 1980.

U2's first album to hit No. 1 in the UK was *War*, which was released in 1983. The singles "Sunday Bloody Sunday" and "Pride (In the Name of Love)" helped U2 build a reputation as a politically and socially conscious band.

In 1987, U2 released their fifth album, which was called *The Joshua Tree*. The album helped them gain international recognition and was considered their biggest success. The singles from the album, "With or Without You" and "I Still Haven't Found What I'm Looking For," are their only songs to have ever hit No. 1 in the United States.

In 2009, the band set off on the U2 360° Tour. The international tour lasted through 2011. The tour was both the highest-grossing and highest-attended concert tour in history!

Since the band's emergence, they've released a total of 14 studio albums and are ranked as one of the world's best-selling music artists of all time. The band has sold more than 170 million records worldwide. They've also won 22 Grammy Awards, which is more than any other band in history. They were inducted into the Rock and Roll Hall of Fame in 2005.

U2's influence on politics and social issues has also been huge. They've done numerous human rights and social justice campaigns.

And to think it all started out in Dublin!

Scenes from *Harry Potter and the Half Blood Prince* Were Filmed at This Irish Attraction

If you're a fan of the *Harry Potter* movie series, then you probably already know that the majority of the scenes from the films were filmed throughout the

United Kingdom, with many scenes taking place in Scotland. But did you know that scenes from *Harry Potter and the Half Blood Prince* were filmed in the Emerald Isle?

When Harry Potter goes on a hunt for Lord Voldemort's Horcruxes, the exterior of the cave was filmed at the Cliffs of Moher, which are located in County Clare, Ireland. This is the only scene in the entire *Harry Potter* movie series that was filmed outside of the United Kingdom.

This isn't the first time the Cliffs of Moher have made an appearance in a film. The cliffs, which are known for their breathtaking beauty, were featured in a number of other movies, too. They were also used as the "Cliffs of Insanity" in *The Princess Bride* and were featured in the movie *Leap Year*, as well as in the movie *Ryans Daughter*. They were also featured in a number of music videos, too, including "Runaway" by Maroon 5, "My Love" by Westlife, and "The Color Green" by Richard Mullin.

A One Direction Band Member is From Ireland

Did you know that Niall Horan of One Direction is Irish? He's the only member of the boy band who's from the Emerald Isle!

Niall Horan was born and raised in Mullingar, Ireland. He attended St. Kenny's National School for elementary school and Coláiste Mhuire, a Catholic all-boys school.

Horan's brother got a guitar for Christmas. When he didn't play it, Niall Horan began to use it and taught himself how to play by watching YouTube when he was just eleven years old.

Niall Horn performed at the Mullingar Arts Centre when he was a teenager.

In 2010 and at the age of sixteen, Niall tried out for the UK show *The X Factor* when tryouts were held in Dublin. For his audition, he sang "So Sick." Although judge Cheryl Cole voted no, judges Simon Cowell and Louis Walsh both voted yes. Horan made it onto the 7th season of the show, thanks to guest judge Katy Perry's yes vote.

At boot camp, Horal didn't qualify for the "Boys" category. Nicole Scherzinger suggested creating a group, which consisted of Niall Horan and four other boys that were also too good to let go. These boys were Harry Styles, Zayn Malik, Liam Payne, and Louis Tomlinson. It was Harry Styles who came up with the name One Direction.

One Direction ended up finishing in third place. They went on to sign with Simon Cowell's record label, Syco Records. Since then, they've gone on to produce hit singles, including "Story of My Life" and "What Makes You Beautiful."

As a solo artist, Niall Horan signed a deal with Capitol Records. His single "Slow Hands" hit No. 7 on the UK Singles Chart, as well as No. 11 on the *Billboard* Hot 100. And it all began with that *X Factor* casting call in Dublin!

Scenes from *Braveheart* Were Filmed in Ireland

If you're a fan of the movie *Braveheart*, then you might be surprised to learn that many scenes from the movie were filmed in Ireland.

The film, which features Mel Gibson as Scottish freedom fighter William Wallace, is set in Scotland. That being said, many of the movie's scenes were filmed in the Emerald Isle. Trim Castle, which is located in County Meath, was used to portray the city of York in *Braveheart*. Trim Castle is the largest Norman Castle located in the Republic of Ireland.

Another scene from the movie was filmed at Bective Abbey. This is the scene in the film where the princess talks with her maid.

Boyne Valley Tours offers a tour with stops at both Bective Abbey and Trim Castle. If you're a *Braveheart* fan, it's something you won't want to miss out on during your next visit to Ireland.

Ed Sheeran Wrote a Song About Ireland

Singer/songwriter Ed Sheeran might be from England, but he definitely has an appreciation for

Ireland. His song "Galway Girl", which just may be the singer's catchiest song to date, is about the Emerald Isle!

Ed Sheeran collaborated with Beoga, an Irish folk band when recording the song "Galway Girl." The song is heavily influenced by Irish folk music, but it also combines both pop and hip-hop in true Sheeran style.

In the song, Ed Sheeran mentions a number of things related to Ireland, including Grafton Street (in Dublin), the Irish folk song "Carrickfergus," fiddles, and more.

Sheeran announced that the song would be the third single from his album on St. Patrick's Day in 2017.

The song hit No. 53 on the US *Billboard* Hot 100, No. 2 on the UK Singles Chart, and No. 1 on the Irish Singles Chart.

This Irish Musician's Song Hit No. 2 on the US *Billboard* Hot 100

Did you know that the song "Take Me to Church" was recorded by an Irish musician? Singer Hozier is from County Wicklow in Leinster, Ireland.

Hozier was born and raised in Bray, Ireland. The musician attended Delgany National School and St. Gerard's School. He eventually went on to study music at Trinity College in Dublin, but he dropped out during his first year to work on his demos for Universal Music.

Hozier's first single "Take Me to Church" peaked at No. 2 on the US *Billboard* Hot 100 in 2013. His debut album, *Hozier*, hit No. 1 in Ireland when it was released in 2014. His single "From Eden" reached No. 2 on the Irish Singles Chart.

Ireland's Bestselling Solo Artist Might Surprise You

Have you ever wondered who Ireland's bestselling solo musician is? You might be surprised to learn that it's the singer Enya!

Enya was raised in Gweedore in County Donegal, a Celtic-speaking area. She was born into a musical family and joined her family's Celtic band Clannad in 1980. At the time, Enya played the keyboard and backup vocals for her family's band. In 1982, however, she left to pursue her own musical career.

Enya's music is heavily influenced by the Celtic culture and folk music. The musician has sung in ten different languages!

In 1984, Enya did soundtrack work for the movie *The Frog Prince*. She also worked on the series *The Celts*, a BBC documentary series, in 1987.

Her hit song "Only Time" was released on her album *A Day Without Rain* in 2000. The song gained a lot of popularity when it was used in the media's portrayal of the 9/11 attacks.

Enya's song "May It Be" was also written for *The Lord of the Rings: The Fellowship of the Ring* in 2001.

In addition to being Ireland's best-selling solo artist, Enya is the second best-selling artist after U2. Enya has sold a total of 75 million records worldwide, including 26.5 million in the United States.

Enya has won four Grammy Awards and seven World Music Awards.

Known for her choice to remain private, Enya has never done a concert tour.

Actor Colin Farrell is From Ireland

Did you know that actor Colin Farrell is from Ireland?

Farrell was born in Castleknock, Dublin, Ireland. He attended St. Brigid's National School, Castleknock College, and Gormanston College.

It was Henry Thomas' performance in the movie *E.T. the Extra-Terrestrial* that inspired Colin Farrell to try out acting. Thomas' performance was so moving that it brought Farrell to tears. Farrell attended the Gaiety School of Acting in Dublin, which led him to his role as Danny Byrne on the BBC drama *Ballykissangel*.

Since then, Colin Farrell has gone on to star in many major box office hits, including *Phone Booth*, *S.W.A.T.*,

The Recruit, Minority Report, Daredevil, Fright Night, and *Horrible Bosses,* to name a few. Farrell earned a Golden Globe Award for Best Action in a Motion Picture Musical or Comedy for his role in the 2008 movie *In Bruges.*

Farrell also starred in the second season of HBO's *True Detective.* He played in *Winter's Tale,* an adaptation of the novel by Mark Helprin. In 2016, Farrell also starred as Percival Graves in *Fantastic Beasts and Where to Find Them,* the *Harry Potter* spin-off.

And to think that it all started out in Ireland!

This Controversial Celebrity is From Ireland

Did you know that singer/songwriter Sinéad O'Connor is from Ireland? The singer, who rose to worldwide fame in the 1990s when she covered Prince's song "Nothing Compares 2 U," was born in Glenageary in County Dublin, Ireland.

When O'Connor was fifteen, she spent 18 months in a Magdalene Asylum after she was charged with shoplifting and truancy.

Sinéad O'Connor isn't only Irish. She's also one of the most controversial artists of all-time!

Sinéad O'Connor has made a number of controversial statements about women's rights, war, child abuse, religion, and other political issues. One of the reasons she's most controversial, however, is due to her ordination as a priest—even though she's a woman.

In another controversial move, Sinéad O'Connor legally changed her name to Magda Davitt in 2017.

This 90s Boyband Was Irish

Did you know that the boyband Westlife was formed in Dublin?

The group was made up of Irish singers Shane Filan, Kian Egan, Markus Feehily, Nicky Byrne, and Brian McFadden. The group was originally signed by Simon Cowell in the UK.

In 1998, Westlife opened for the Backstreet Boys when they performed in Dublin. The following April, they released their first single "Swear It Again." The song quickly hit No. 1 on both the UK and Irish Singles Charts. It is their one and only song that ever hit the US *Billboard* Hot 100, where it reached No. 20.

The group sold more than 40 million studio albums and 55 million records across the globe. Fourteen of the group's singles hit No.1 in the UK.

As of 2012, Westlife was the 34th biggest-selling singles artist and 16th biggest-selling group in the history of British music. They also currently hold the *Guinness World Records* for multiple records, including the first to have seven consecutive singles in the UK. As well as the most singles to debut at the

No. 1 spot on the UK chart, and the top-selling album group in the UK during the 21st century.

Westlife has had more than a million views on YouTube and more than half a million streams on Spotify.

In 2011, Westlife split. In October of 2018, however, the band announced that they were reuniting for a tour and new music. Their new single, which was written by Ed Sheeran, is expected to be released in late 2018. Will this be the band's big comeback? Time will tell!

Liam Neeson's Career Started Out in the Emerald Isle

Did you know that actor Liam Neeson is from the Emerald Isle?

Liam Neeson was born in Ballymena, Country Antrim, Northern Island. He later went on to perform for the Lyric Players' Theatre in Belfast for two years. He landed his first role in a region film called *Pilgrim's Progress* in 1978. The same year, Neeson moved to Dublin where he played in *Says I, Say He* at the Project Arts Centre.

Neeson later went on to join the Abbey Theatre. He starred in Brian Friel's *Translations* in 1980.

Filmmaker John Boorman recognized Neeson's potential when he saw him perform as Lennie in the play *Of Mice and Men.* Boorman offered him a role in the movie *Excalibur.*

Once the movie was filmed, Neeson moved to London. His roommate was Helen Mirren, who he'd met while working on *Excalibur.*

After that, Neeson went on to star in *The Bounty* with Mel Gibson and Anthony Hopkins, *The Mission* with Robert De Niro and Jeremy Irons, and *Next of Kin* with Patrick Swayze.

In 1993, Neeson played the lead role in *Schindler's List.* He has since played in *Les Misérables, Star Wars: Episode 1—The Phantom Menace, Batman Begins,* and the TV series *Taken.* Neeson also did the voice of Aslan in *The Chronicles of Narnia* and the monster in *A Monster Calls.*

Neeson has also won a number of awards throughout the course of his career, including an Academy Award for Best Actor and three Golden Globe Awards for Best Actor in a Motion Picture Drama.

And it all started out in the Emerald Isle!

Game of Thrones is Filmed in Ireland

Did you know that HBO's *Game of Thrones* is filmed in the Emerald Isle?

The show, which is based on George R. R. Martin's book series *A Song of Ice and Fire,* is set in the fictional continents of Westeros and Essos. But in real life, Belfast and other locations throughout Northern Ireland have frequently been used for film locations.

Although the show is filmed in other countries as well, some of its most iconic scenes were filmed in Ireland. The Glens of Antrim provided the backdrop for the Riverlands that Sansa and Baelish crossed in the show. Portstewart Strand was used to portray Dorne. Castle Ward in County Down, Northern Ireland was also used as a film location for a scene in *Game of Thrones.*

This Iconic Actress Was Irish-American

Today, she's recognized as one of the most iconic actresses and greatest talents of all time. But did you know that Maureen O'Hara was Irish-American?

Born as Maureen FitzSimons, the actress was born on Beechwood Avenue in Ranelagh in Dublin, Ireland. *My Irish Molly* is the only film she ever made under her real name. O'Hara later became her stage name because it was easier to remember. She became American thanks to marriage.

O'Hara wanted to be an actress from a young age. When she was 10 years old, O'Hara trained at the Rathmines Theater Company. At the age of 14, she trained at the Abbey Theatre. Charles Loughton saw her potential and got her a role with him in Alfred Hitchcock's *Jamaica Inn* in 1939.

That same year, O'Hara moved to Hollywood to star alongside Laughton in *The Hunchback of Notre Dame*.

She signed a contract with RKO Pictures and the rest is history. She soon earned the nickname of "The Queen of Technicolor" and went on to star in many major films.

In 1961, Maureen O'Hara starred as one of her most beloved roles. She played the mother to actress Hayley Mills in the *Disney* film *The Parent Trap*. The movie was about twins separated at birth who meet at summer camp and scheme to get their divorced parents back together.

The famous redheaded actress frequently starred in movies alongside her longtime friend John Wayne. Their first movie together was *Rio Grande*. They also starred in *The Quiet Man*, which was recorded in Ireland, and one of O'Hara's most well-known movies, *The Wings of Eagles*. The last film they starred in together was *Big Jake* in 1971.

John Wayne and Maureen O'Hara remained friends until he died of cancer in 1979. After his death, she fell into a deep depression.

In 1991, Maureen O'Hara did one more film called *Only in the Lonely*, in which she starred alongside John Candy.

Until her death in 2015, Maureen O'Hara was one of

the last surviving actors from the Golden Age of Hollywood.

This Former *James Bond* Actor is From Ireland

Did you know the fifth actor to portray James Bond is from Ireland?

Pierce Brosnan played James Bond in 1995 in the movie *GoldenEye*. He later resumed the role in the movies *Tomorrow Never Dies, The World is Not Enough*, and *Die Another Day*.

Brosnan was born in Drogheda, County Louth and spent most of his childhood in Nava, County Meath, Ireland. His mother moved to London to work as a nurse when he was four. She left Pierce in Ireland where he was raised by his maternal grandparents and then later an aunt and an uncle before being sent to live in a boarding house.

Brosnan eventually left Ireland to be reunited with his mother and stepfather, who were living in Scotland. His stepfather took him to see his first James Bond film—*Goldfinger*—when he was 11 years old.

Brosnan later moved to London where he attended school. Brosnan has said that he felt like an outsider as an Irish boy when he was going to school in London. The kids bullied him there and called him "Irish" as a nickname.

After leaving school at 16, he went on to work for a circus for three years and then later trained for acting for three years at the Drama Centre London.

After stage acting, he earned his first role in the TV series *Remington Steele*. He's went on to play in *The Fourth Protocol*, *Mrs. Doubtfire*, *The Ghost Writer*, *The November Man*, *The Matador*, and *Mama Mia!* For many fans, however, Brosnan is most remembered for his role as James Bond!

RANDOM FACTS

1. Jonathan Swift, the author of *Gulliver's Travels*, was born in Dublin, Ireland. He came from a family with literary connections, which included John Dryden, Sir Walter Raleigh, and Francis Goodwin.

2. Ireland's *Late Late Show* is the 2nd longest running late-night talk show in the world. It's surpassed only by the United States' *The Tonight Show*.

3. The 90s boy band Boyzone was from Ireland. They had a total of 21 singles on the top 40 UK charts and 22 singles that topped the Irish charts.

4. The film *King Arthur*, starring Kiera Knightley and Clive Owen, was filmed in Ireland. Some of the scenes were shot at Ardmore Studios in County Wicklow and Ballymore Eustace in County Kildare.

5. Colin Farrell auditioned for Boyzone, but he wasn't chosen to be a part of the band.

6. The cult classic film *Excalibur* was filmed entirely in Ireland. Cahir Castle in Tipperary was used for one of the movie's epic battle scenes. Powerscourt Waterfall and the woodlands in county Wicklow were also used for filming. Today, fans of the

movie can take "Excalibur Drive" around Wicklow to see locations that were used throughout the film.

7. *Far and Away*, starring Nicole Kidman and Tom Cruise, was filmed in Ireland. Film locations included the Dingle Peninsula and Inch Strand.

8. The Oscar-winning film *Ryan's Daughter* was filmed in Ireland, with film locations including Dingle Peninsula and Inch Strand as well.

9. W.B. Yeats was an Irish poet. He also served for two terms as Senator of the Irish Free State. Yeats was born in Sandymount, Ireland.

10. The novel *Ulysses* was written by Irish novelist and poet James Joyce. *Ulysses* is set in Dublin.

11. The TV series *Vikings* is filmed in Ireland. Most of the show is filmed in the Wicklow Mountains in Leinster, thanks to the area's resemblance to Scandinavia, where the show is set. Lough Tay and Powerscourt Demesne are used in scenes in the show.

12. Dublin native Gabriel Byrne played as a local chieftain in *Vikings*! Byrne has played in a number of other films, including *Excalibur, Stigmata, End of Days*, and *Vampire Academy.*

13. Scenes from the show *Penny Dreadful* were filmed in Ireland. Dublin is used in place of Victorian London. Dublin Castle, Merrion Square, Temple

Bar, and the Kings Inns (a historic law school) have all been used throughout the show.

14. The 2005 movie *Lassie* was filmed in Ireland. The Macgillycuddy Reeks mountain range in County Kerry, Ireland was used as a backdrop for the film.

15. The TV series *The Tudors* was filmed entirely in the Emerald Isle. Ardmore Studios in County Wicklow was used for the entire four-season series.

16. *The Tudors* actor Jonathan Rhys Meyers was born in Dublin, Ireland. Meyers has also starred in other major films, including *Bend It Like Beckham*, *Match Point*, *Mission: Impossible III*, and *The Mortal Instruments: City of Bones*.

17. Saoirse Ronan is an Irish-American actress. While she was born in New York City, her parents are both from Dublin. Ronan got her big break in the movie *The Lovely Bones*, which is based on the novel of the same name by Alice Sebold.

18. Actress Evanna Lynch was born in Termonfeckin, County Louth, Ireland. She's best-known for her role as Luna Lovegood in the *Harry Potter* movie series.

19. Fiona Shaw is an Irish actress who played Harry's Aunt Petunia in the *Harry Potter* movie series. Shaw was born in County Cork.

20. Actress Sarah Bolger is from Dublin. Bolger is most well-known for playing Lady Mary Tudor in *The Tudors* and Princess Aurora in *Once Upon a Time*.

Test Yourself – Questions

1. *Harry Potter and the Half Blood Prince*, *The Princess Bride*, and *Leap Year* all had scenes filmed at:

   a. The Macgillycuddy Reeks
   b. The Wicklow Mountains
   c. The Cliffs of Moher

2. Ireland's best-selling solo artist of all-time is:

   a. Ed Sheeran
   b. Enya
   c. Bono

3. Which show is <u>not</u> filmed in Ireland?

   a. *Once Upon a Time*
   b. *The Tudors*
   c. *Game of Thrones*

4. Which iconic actress is from Ireland?

   a. Lucille Ball
   b. Marilyn Monroe
   c. Maureen O'Hara

5. Which 90s boy band was <u>not</u> from Ireland?

   a. Boyzone
   b. O-Town
   c. Westlife

Answers

1. c.

2. b.

3. a.

4. c.

5. b.

CHAPTER THREE

ST. PATRICK'S DAY, LEPRECHAUNS, AND MORE!

When you think of Ireland, Saint Patrick's Day may be one of the first things that comes to mind. The holiday is celebrated by millions of people throughout the world. But how much do you really know about the holiday? Do you know who St. Patrick was? Do you know what shamrocks have to do with the holiday? Do you know where the first St. Patrick's Day Parade took place? To find out the answers to these questions and more, read on!

St. Patrick's Day is Celebrated Differently in Ireland

Around the world and in the United States, in particular, St. Patrick's Day is celebrated mostly by drinking beer. Green beer, mostly, and lots of it. To say that St. Patrick's Day is celebrated somewhat differently in Ireland would be a bit of an understatement.

St. Patrick's Day has traditionally been celebrated as both a religious and cultural holiday in Ireland. The holiday celebrates Christianity's arrival in Ireland.

Celebrated on March 17th, St. Patrick's Day in Ireland generally involves attending mass at some point during the day. Traditionally, this day was meant to be spent in prayer and reflection. It wasn't a day to go to the pub. For Roman Catholic people, it's a holy day of obligation.

St. Patrick's Day has been celebrated in Ireland since the 17th century. For the majority of the 20th century, pubs were actually closed on March 17th. At that point, St. Patrick's Day was only considered a religious holiday in Ireland. It wasn't until 1970 that St. Patrick's Day officially became a national holiday and pubs were able to open for business again. Nowadays, many people in Ireland do go to the pubs for a few drinks—*after* they go to church.

The Irish also do celebrate by wearing green and shamrocks, the same way Americans do. St. Patrick's Day parades weren't commonplace in Ireland at one point, but American influence has led the country to partake in this holiday tradition.

St. Patrick Wasn't Irish

It might shock you to learn that St. Patrick wasn't Irish. He was actually born in Great Britain, though historians aren't sure whether he was born in England, Wales or Scotland. His parents were Roman.

St. Patrick's past was a tragic one. He was kidnapped when he was sixteen years old by Irish raiders. He was thrust into slavery and forced to work as a sheepherder. After six years, he managed to escape Ireland and returned home.

St. Patrick Brought Christianity With Him

So, now that you know St. Patrick wasn't Irish, you're probably wondering why the holiday is named after him. What could he have to do with the Emerald Isle's most famed holiday?

When St. Patrick is credited with bringing Christianity to Ireland.

After he escaped Ireland and returned home, he studied to become an ordained priest. He eventually returned to Ireland as a missionary. He converted many of Ireland's pagans to Christianity. It's believed that Patrick began to introduce Christianity to the Emerald Isle in the year 432 A.D. It's been said that he baptized hundreds of people in just one day.

St. Patrick Wasn't Even His Real Name, and His Sainthood Has Also Been Questioned

Did you know that St. Patrick's real name wasn't even Patrick?

The name that was given to him at birth was Maewyn Succat. It wasn't until when he became a priest that he took on the name Patrick.

In addition, people have also questioned whether or not St. Patrick was an actual Saint. This is because St. Patrick was never officially canonized (or declared a saint only on those who the Pope found worthy of the title). However, it wasn't until *after* St. Patrick's death that the practice of canonizing saints was adopted. In those times, the title was used to recognize people who had holy lives or performed martyr-like acts.

But the Holiday Falls on the Day of His Death

Regardless of whether or not St. Patrick was actually a saint or not, St. Patrick's Day is celebrated on March 17th, the day St. Patrick allegedly died. When exactly did St. Patrick die?

Well, no one really knows for sure. Historians haven't been able to determine what year St. Patrick died during. Some believe that his death may have been in the year 460 A.D., while others believe he may have lived until 493 A.D., which would have made him 120 years old. Despite the controversy over which year he died during, most historians generally accept March 17th as the date of his death.

It is known that St. Patrick died in the first church he built in Saul, Downpatrick, Ireland.

Green Actually Has Nothing to Do with St. Patrick

Many people associate the color green with St. Patrick's Day. From green clothes to green beer, you might be wondering what the significance of green is to the holiday.

Well, I hate to be the bearer of bad news, but there is no significance. In fact, according to historians, light blue is the color that would best represent the holiday, if anything. In the earliest depictions of St. Patrick, he was usually wearing light blue undergarments. Light blue was associated with Ireland in general during those times.

Red also doesn't have anything to do with the earliest records of leprechauns, either, who were believed to wear red.

So, where did green come from? During the 1798 Irish Rebellion, the clover became a symbol of Irish nationalism. It's believed that this is why the color has become so closely associated with St. Patrick's Day.

The First St. Patrick's Day Parade Took Place Here

If you ever envisioned the first St. Patrick's Day parade taking place in Ireland, you were wrong!

The first St. Patrick's Day parade was actually held in

America. In 1762, the first St. Patrick's Day parade was held in New York City. Irish soldiers who were serving in the English army paraded through New York City streets.

Today, the St. Patrick's Day Parade in New York City is one the largest parades in the entire world. An estimated 150,000 people march in the parade, which generally sees about 2 million spectators. The parade goes up Fifth Avenue, spanning from East 44th Street to East 79th Street. The parade's marchers walk entirely by foot. Floats, cars, and other modern technologies aren't allowed.

Ireland didn't have its first St. Patrick's Day parade until 1903. The first parade in honor of the holiday took place in Waterford.

Leprechauns Have No Actual Connection to St. Patrick's Day

St. Patrick's Day celebrations around the globe often include the leprechauns, a red-haired mythical little man with a pot of gold. Known for their mischief, leprechauns are one of the most well-known symbols of St. Patrick's Day. Have you ever wondered what leprechauns have to do with Ireland's most famous Saint?

The answer may surprise you. Leprechauns have absolutely nothing to do with St. Patrick himself. So, why have we all embraced the idea of these mythical beings played such a big role in Ireland's most famous holiday? For most of us, it's hard to imagine Patrick's Day without leprechauns.

Leprechauns are simply one of Ireland's most famous folklore. They have become a symbol of the holiday the same way reindeer or elves are associated with Christmas. It's believed that there's no rhyme or reason for how the leprechaun came to play such an integral role in St. Patrick's Day, but it sure makes the holiday a lot more fun—especially for kids!

Leprechauns Are Actually Believed to Be Fairies

Historians believe that leprechauns—a word which originates from an Irish word meaning "small-bodied fellow—came from the Celtic concept of fairies. According to Celtic lore, there were tiny men and women who possessed magical powers and were tricksters.

Leprechauns are considered to be a part of the fairy family. They're small and mischievous. It's believed that leprechauns lived in Ireland long before humans did.

You might be wondering why there are only said to be male leprechauns when fairies can be either male or female. One legend says that leprechauns are the unwanted fairies who have been disowned by the other fairies. This also explains why leprechauns are said to be grouchy, untrusting, and lonely creatures.

According to historians, the idea of leprechauns actually originated from real people. When the Gaelic invaded Ireland during the 5th century B.C., they found a race of men who were about five feet tall. The Gaelic invaders called them "little people."

Legends About Leprechauns

You've probably heard that leprechauns have gold, but do you know why the little men are thought to be rich?

There are several theories. Leprechauns are said to craft shoes and can be heard from the tapping sound of the hammer they use to make shoes with. According to some legends, the shoes are what makes leprechauns rich. Other tales say that leprechauns serve as protectors of the fairy world's treasure, while others believe they act as bankers.

Legend says that if you catch a leprechaun, he will be compelled to tell you the truth and take you to the secret spot where he's hiding his pot of gold. If you ever find yourself fortunate enough to catch a leprechaun, however, it's important to make sure that you don't take your eyes off of him or he will disappear.

It's said that a leprechaun's pot of gold is hidden at

the end of a rainbow. Since people can't find the end of the rainbow, the only way they can reach the gold is if a leprechaun takes them there.

Leprechauns are also said to show kindness when it's shown to them. In one particular legend, a struggling nobleman let a leprechaun ride on his horse. When the nobleman returned to his castle, the leprechaun had filled it to the ceiling with gold.

Another popular legend says that if a leprechaun is captured by a human, he will grant them three wishes in exchange for his freedom.

People Try to Catch Leprechauns on St. Patrick's Day

Due to all of the legends surrounding leprechauns being captured by a human, people around the globe—but especially in the United States—try to catch leprechauns on St. Patrick's Day.

People leprechaun-sized traps. In an attempt at luring the leprechaun, they lay out pennies or chocolate coins. The shininess of the penny or the chocolate coin wrapper is thought to lure the leprechaun.

The tradition, which is most comparable to leaving out cookies for Santa Claus on Christmas Eve, are generally made for families with young children.

How the Shamrock Ties into St. Patrick's Day

Have you ever wondered what shamrocks have to do with St. Patrick's Day? Unlike leprechauns, shamrocks actually *are* relevant to the holiday.

Shamrocks, or three-leaved clovers, have been used as an Irish symbol since the 18th century. The word shamrock originates from the Irish word "seamróg," which translates to "little clover."

It's believed that St. Patrick used the shamrock when he converted the Irish to Christianity. He used the three leaves of the clover to explain the concept of the Holy Trinity. Each leaf represented the Father, the Son, and the Holy Spirit.

It became a St. Patrick's Day tradition to wear a shamrock on your lapel at the end of the 17th century. The tradition became widespread after it came to be recognized as a national emblem during the Irish fight for independence.

Shamrock Leaves Are Said to Have Lucky Meanings

The shamrock is often confused with the four-leaf clover. Since four-leaf clovers are difficult to find in nature, it's been said that finding one is good luck. It's been estimated that there's only one four-leaf clover for every 10,000 three-leaf clovers. Due to their rarity, four-leaf clovers are considered to be one of the most popular good luck symbols in the United States, where it's not uncommon for four-leaf clovers to be used in place of three-leaf clovers on St. Patrick's Day.

The four leaves are widely believed to be symbolic of hope, faith, love, and luck! Some also believe that the leaves symbolize fame, wealth, love, and health.

In Ireland, five-leaf clovers—known as "rose clovers"—are said to bring even more luck.

The Surprising Meaning of "Luck of the Irish"

If you've ever heard the phrase "luck of the Irish," you probably think it means "good fortune." It makes sense with all of the leprechauns that are said to be roaming the Emerald Isle. This meaning couldn't be further from the truth, however. The term didn't even originate from Ireland and its origins are actually quite derogatory.

The phrase came about during the American gold and silver rush during the later half of the 19th century. Many of the miners who were the most successful were Irish immigrants or Irish-American. They were rejected on the east coast and moved west where they found gold and silver.

People—Native Americans, especially—despised the Irish because of these successes. People refused to believe that the Irish found gold or silver because they were smart enough. The expression "luck of the Irish" was a sarcastic, undermining or mocking way to say that the Irish miners could only succeed thanks to luck, rather than brains or hard work.

Today, the phrase is commonly associated with St. Patrick's Day and leprechauns, however.

RANDOM FACTS

1. It's been estimated that 5.5 million pints of Guinness beer are sold throughout the world on a daily basis, but nearly 15 million pints are sold internationally on St. Patrick's Day. In the United States alone, an average of 600,000 pints of Guinness is sold on a daily basis, but a whopping 3 million is downed on the Irish holiday.

2. According to *ABC*, Guinness isn't the most popular beer that's drunk on St. Patrick's Day in the United States. Samuel Adams ranked in at No. 1 with Corona Extra ranking in at No. 2.

3. An estimated $245 million is spent on beer across the globe on the holiday.

4. The first American St. Patrick's Day celebration took place in 1737 in Boston, Massachusetts.

5. It has been said that there are 236 leprechauns that live in the caverns of Carlingford Mountain in County Louth, Ireland. The EU has apparently granted heritage status to the leprechauns that are believed to live there. In addition to the sanctuary for the leprechauns, animals and plants in the area are also protected.

6. The traditional St. Patrick's Day meal of corned beef and cabbage doesn't contain corn. The term

comes from the large grains of salt that were once used to cure meat, which was referred to as "corns."

7. Historically, corned beef was *not* eaten in Ireland. In fact, it was unheard of (though the salt-cured beef was eaten on occasion by the Irish). Pork was a lot cheaper to raise and eat for the average Irish family. The tradition of eating corned beef on St. Patrick's Day didn't begin until the end of the 19th century. The tradition began in America where Irish immigrants living in New York City bought corned beef from Jewish delis. The beef was affordable and many of the immigrants were poor. Over time, it became accepted throughout the United States as traditional Irish fare—even though it's not.

8. On St. Patrick's Day, the Irish prime minister presents the President of the United States with a crystal bowl of shamrocks. It's viewed as a symbol of the close ties between Ireland and the USA. The tradition dates back to the 1950s. However, in 2010, it was revealed that the shamrocks must be destroyed as part of the Secret Service's policy.

9. The world's shortest St. Patrick's Day parade used to be held in Dripsey in County Cork, Ireland. The parade was just 77 feet long, which was the distance between two pubs: The Lee

Valley and The Weigh Inn. But today, the town of Hot Springs, Arkansas allegedly has the shortest St. Patrick's Day parade in the world. The 98-foot parade takes place on Bridge Street.

10. In Chicago, Illinois, the Plumbers Local 110 union celebrates St. Patrick's Day by dyeing the Chicago River a shade of Kelly green. It takes 40 tons of dye to get the river to turn green, and it stays that way for about five hours.

11. Irish Catholics are given a reprieve from Lent practices, like fasting, on St. Patrick's Day. When St. Patrick's Day falls on a Friday, Catholic-practicing Catholics are given permission to eat corned beef instead of going meatless during Lent.

12. St. Patrick's Day is celebrated all around the world—and even in space! In fact, the holiday has been celebrated several times on NASA's International Space Station. Back in 2013, Canadian astronaut Chris Hadfield filmed herself singing "Danny Boy" on March 17th. Two years prior to that, the flute was played in the satellite by astronaut Cady Coleman for St. Patrick's Day.

13. St. Patrick isn't the only patron saint of Ireland. Saint Brigid and Saint Columba's remains were later buried with St. Patrick's at his final resting place in Downpatrick.

14. A popular legend about St. Patrick is that he eliminated all of the snakes and toads from Ireland. This is nothing more than a myth. Due to Ireland's glacial history and geographical location, the country didn't have snakes to begin with. St. Patrick likely gained the reputation of a snake exterminator because he converted Ireland's pagans to Christianity and pagan spiritual beliefs and practices were often considered "snake-like."

15. Dublin's first official, state-sponsored St. Patrick's Day parade didn't place until 1931!

16. The largest celebrations of the holiday take place in Downpatrick, County Down because it's St. Patrick's burial spot.

17. Many view eating green food on St. Patrick's Day is actually considered culturally insensitive. Due to the harsh conditions of the Irish Potato Famine, people resorted to eating grass. It's been said that people's mouths were green when they died from eating the grass. If you decide to serve green food on St. Patrick's Day, it might be a good time for a history lesson!

18. The term "Pinch me, I'm Irish" is a purely American tradition that's believed to have started in the 1700s. It was said that wearing green made you invisible to leprechauns. If you didn't wear green, you risked getting pinched

by a leprechaun. If you forget to wear green on St. Patrick's Day and you feel someone pinch you, it just may have been a leprechaun.

19. A number of movies have been made about St. Patrick's Day. Some of these films are horror films, while others are family-friendly. Some movies based on the holiday include *Leprechaun*, *The Luck of the Irish*, *Muck*, and *Red Clover*.

20. There's a constant debate over whether it's St. Patty's Day or St. Paddy's Day. Many argue that it's St. Paddy's Day because the English-name, Patrick, stems from the Irish Gaelic name, Pádraig. The abbreviation for Pádraig would be "Paddy," while "Patty" is used more often in Ireland as an abbreviation for the name Patricia. But to make things more confusing, "Pat" is also used as an abbreviation for Patrick.

Test Yourself – Questions

1. St. Patrick's parents were:

   a. Scottish
   b. Roman
   c. English

2. "The luck of the Irish" originated from America during:

   a. The Civil War
   b. The formation of the Hollywood movie industry
   c. The Gold and Silver Rush

3. On St. Patrick's Day, how much Guinness beer is sold across the world?

   a. Nearly 5 million pints
   b. Nearly 15 million pints
   c. Nearly 50 million pints

4. Leprechauns are believed to be closely related to which mythological creature?

   a. Elves
   b. vampires
   c. fairies

5. Which American city dyes their river green in celebration of St. Patrick's Day?

   a. Chicago
   b. Boston
   c. New York City

Answers

1. b.

2. c.

3. b.

4. c.

5. a.

CHAPTER FOUR

IRELAND'S INVENTIONS, IDEAS, AND MORE!

Have you ever wondered what inventions you can thank Ireland for? Do you know which products from your daily life were invented in or produced by the Emerald Isle? Do you know which popular junk food came from Ireland? Do you know how Bailey's Irish Cream was invented? Do you know which medical equipment was invented in the state? In this chapter, you'll find out what inventions, ideas, and products originated from the Irish.

Color Photography

Today, it's difficult to imagine a world in which color photography didn't exist. We use photos to capture memories, landscapes, and sell business products. Well, it might surprise you to learn that you can thank an Irishman for the invention!

John Joly, who lived near Bracknagh in County

Offaly, attended Trinity College where he studied engineering.

Back in 1894, Joly designed a color photography system. His concept was based on taking viewing plates with narrow lines in three colors. The viewing plate would be marked with thin colored lines. The plate would be placed in the camera in the front of the camera.

It turned out that Joly's method was effective. Since it was also easier to use than any other type of color photography technologies that came before his invention, he's credited with the first "practical" method of color photography. Joly's then-innovative technology paved the way for the color photography that we see on a daily basis today.

Flavored Potato Crisps

Today, potato crisps come in all sort of flavors, ranging from Sour Cream and Onion to Ketchup. But have you ever wondered who thank for potato crisps or, as the Americans know them, potato chips?

The credit goes to Dublin native Joseph "Spud" Murphy. Back in the 1950s, Murphy hated the taste of plain potato crisps. At the time, the only flavor offered was salt. Sure, there are salt-flavored potato crisps that taste just fine today, but back then you were given a packet of salt that you had to pour over the potato crisps. Murphy would have told you that they weren't very good.

Thanks to his hatred of the crisps, Murphy opened a potato crisp company of his own back in 1954. Located in the Republic of Ireland, the company was named Tayto.

Murphy started out his business at the O'Rahilly Parade in Dublin. He started with just eight workers out of a van.

One of the workers, Seamus Burke, experimented with different flavor options until he found one that Murphy approved of. The flavor was cheese and onion.

Murphy was unsure of how to market the invention, but he approached the Findlater family, who owned 21 upscale grocery and wine stores in the Republic of Ireland. Not only did they sell the flavored potato crisps in their stores, but they also sold them to other outlets.

Today, Tayto is one of the most widely recognized brands in all of Ireland.

The Submarine

Did you know that the Submarine was invented by an Irishman? Today it's recognized as one of Ireland's greatest inventions, even though it was in the United States that the Submarine was really invented.

John Philip Holland of Liscannor County is responsible for the Submarine. Holland immigrated to Boston, Massachusetts back in 1872. It was there that he tested out his first prototype. Unfortunately, it sank immediately after being launched.

In 1881, the Fenian Brotherhood funded Holland's model, the "Fenian Ram." The model was a huge success.

The U.S. Naval Department offered competitions to design and build submarines. Holland was the winner of three of those competitions.

After successful trials of Holland's model—the "Holland VII"—the United States Navy purchased its first submarine for him. They went on to purchase six more of Holland's submarines.

Holland's invention changed both naval warfare and underwater exploration forever!

The Binaural Stethoscope

Did you know that one of the most essential tools in modern medicine was invented by a Wexford, Ireland native?

The original stethoscope was actually invented by a man named Rene Laennec from France in 1819. However, a Wexford native by the name of Arthur Leared came to the realization that the stethoscope could be more effective than it was. Leared used rubber tubes to connect two earpieces to the cylinder.

The first time the binaural stethoscope was displayed was at the Great Exhibition in London in 1851. Leared's invention received a lot of praise. His design paved the way to the stethoscope we all know of today.

The Hypodermic Syringe

Did you know that the hypodermic syringe was invented by an Irish doctor? The hypodermic needle, which is commonly used for injection and local anesthetics today, was invented by a Dublin doctor named Francis Rynd.

Dr. Rynd was a surgeon at Meath Hospital in Dublin. The hospital was a popular place for research and training. While many medical inventions came out of the hospital, Rynd's hypodermic syringe is by far one of the most important.

Dr. Rynd's invention came about when a woman who had been suffering from facial pain due to neuralgia didn't respond to drinking morphine.

In 1844, Rynd designed the hypodermic needle, which he used to place the morphine under the woman's skin, essentially giving her a powerful local anesthetic.

Rynd's syringe was made from a small tube and a cutting device known as a trocar. He used the trocar to puncture the skin on the woman's face. The morphine flowed through the cannula and under her skin.

Rynd's invention turned out to be effective. After the injection, the woman was able to sleep well for the first time in months.

Rynd's new technology became a common pain relief method. Florence Nightingale was one of the first to be treated with it during an illness.

The plunger syringe was later invented in 1853.

Seismology

Ireland might not seem like a place where you'd expect the scientific study of earthquakes to be born. But alas, you can thank an Irishman for the invention of seismology, which is the study of earthquakes and elastic waves that move through the earth.

Today, seismologists study earthquakes and related phenomena, such as tsunamis. They use instruments called seismographs, which they use to monitor the earth's crust. Seismologists evaluate the potential dangers of earthquakes and how to minimize the potential dangers they pose.

The idea of seismology was first posed by Robert Mallet, who is today known as the "father of seismology." Mallet was a geophysicist from Dublin, who did his studies at Trinity College, Dublin. A paper that Mallet wrote back in 1846, which was titled *On the Dynamics of Earthquakes*, is considered the basis on which modern-day seismology was founded.

Not only did Mallet write several papers that helped scientists better understand the science of earthquakes, but he also came up with the terms, "seismology" and "epicenter."

Modern Stamps

Some people collect them, while others loathe how much they cost. Whether you love them or hate them, modern-day postage stamps were invented by an Irishman.

When stamps first came about, they were originally printed on rectangular sheets of paper. You had to use scissors to cut stamps from the sheets, which often led to crooked edges.

Fortunately, Henry Archer came up with a solution. Archer, who was an Irish businessman living in London at the time, created a perforation machine. His machine perforated sheets of stamps, which gave stamps the rippled outline that we're all familiar with today.

In 1850, the Penny Red became the first stamp to ever be perforated.

The Emergency Defibrillator

There's no doubt that the emergency defibrillator is one of the most life-saving pieces of medical equipment in hospitals today. We can thank Professor Frank Pantridge, who was a doctor from Northern Ireland for the invention.

Pantridge, who was from County Down, was a cardiologist. In 1957, Pantridge introduced CPR to the Royal Victoria Hospital in Belfast, Ireland. However, Pantridge quickly realized that many people died from ventricular fibrillation, which needed to be treated as soon as possible.

He first introduced the mobile coronary care unit, which was an ambulance with special equipment and staff who could provide care for patients before they arrived at the hospital.

Pantridge later developed the portable defibrillator. The first emergency defibrillator was installed in a Belfast ambulance in 1965. The first version weighed 70 kg and ran on car batteries. By 1968, however, Pantridge had come up with a new design that weighed only 3 kg. It included a miniature capacitor. The new model was manufactured for NASA.

Rubber-Soled Shoes

Today, we take rubber-soled shoes for granted. Did you know that rubber-soled shoes started out in the Emerald Isle?

Humphrey O'Sullivan was an Irish immigrant from Skibbereen, County Cork, Ireland who worked in the United States at a printing press in Lowell, Massachusetts in the late 1890s. O'Sullivan found himself in a lot of foot pain after standing all day.

The idea for his invention was born when he stood on a rubber matt, which he used as a cushion. He found that the rubber matt helped relieved his foot pain. Once his co-workers caught on, they even began stealing the matt from him to try to ease their own feet pain.

O'Sullivan cut two pieces from the mat the size of his heels and nailed them to the bottom of his shoes. He was very happy with the results of his idea.

Shortly after he came up with the idea, O'Sullivan began to make full rubber heels, using hidden washers to hold the nails in place. It was the first rubber heels to have ever been made. O'Sullivan began to sell them to the shoemakers in the area.

Within a few years, O'Sullivan's heels began to be shipped all over the country and his invention earned the name of "America's No. 1 Heel". While his product was first manufactured at the Boston Belting Company, they were soon picked up by Goodrich Rubber Company in Akron, Ohio.

Chocolate Milk *and* Milk Chocolate

Chocolate milk and milk chocolate are arguably two of the best inventions in the world (unless you're lactose intolerant, of course). But if you're like the rest of the world who grew up with a love for chocolate milk and who looks forward to milk chocolate at just about every holiday, then you might be wondering who to credit for the inventions. Well, you can thank an Irishman, who invented both chocolate milk *and* milk chocolate!

During the 1660s, Hans Sloan was a Killyleagh, County Down, Northern Ireland native during the 17th century. Sloan later went on to become a physician. At one point, he was studying in Jamaica. It was while he was there that he came up with the idea of chocolate milk. Sloan noticed the native Jamaicans mixing cocoa with water. When Sloan tried the concoction himself, he didn't think it tasted good. In fact, he even found it nauseating.

Inspired by their mixture, Sloan tried to come up with a concoction of his own. He added cocoa to milk and found that it tasted a little better. It might surprise you to learn, however, that Sloan didn't originally sell his cocoa-milk mixture just for drinking purposes.

When Sloan later moved to England, he took the recipe with him and sold it to an apothecary as a medicine. It was used to treat digestion and consumption.

Later, Sloan went on to boil cocoa with milk and sugar. His invention was milk chocolate. Cadbury began to produce his invention, which was first sold as "Sir Hans Sloane's Milk Chocolate."

Bailey's Irish Cream

It might not surprise you to learn that Bailey's Irish Cream was invented in Ireland. It was developed by Gilbeys of Ireland, which is a division of International Distillers & Vintners. In 1971, the company decided it wanted to create a product that it could market internationally.

A man by the name of Mac Macpherson, who worked in the Gilbeys research laboratory during the 1970s, was tasked with inventing the drink. Macpherson was told that the company would be starting a new brand of drinks for exportation. He wasn't given any details on what type of drink he was to invent, only that it needed to contain alcohol.

Macpherson and one of his colleagues managed to invent Bailey's Irish Cream within 45 minutes.

Macpherson came up with the idea of incorporating Ireland's reputation as a dairy producer into the drink. From there, his colleague came up with the idea of mixing Irish whiskey and cream.

They bought a bottle of Jameson's Irish Whiskey and a tub of cream, which they mixed together in their kitchen. Although they felt the mixture had potential, it didn't taste that good. They added sugar, which was an improvement but they felt that it was still missing something. The final ingredient they added was Cadbury's Powdered Drinking Chocolate — and they found themselves astounded at how good it was. They also felt that the cream seemed to give the alcohol a stronger taste.

The following year, in 1974, Bailey's Irish Cream was introduced as the first Irish cream on the market.

Since the drink was released onto the market, more than a billion bottles have been sold. You might think that Macpherson and his colleague are rich thanks to their invention, but that simply isn't the case. They were only paid about £3,000 for their invention.

The whiskey and cream-based liqueur, which has an alcohol content of 17%, is produced in Dublin and Mallusk, Northern Ireland today.

Tattoo Machines

Estimates have found that 21% of the world's population or approximately one in five adults have tattoos. There's a good chance that you may even have one yourself. From butterflies to tribal symbols, tattoos are a popular form of art today. Did you know that, while it was not invented in Ireland, the modern tattoo machine was invented by an Irishman?

Samuel O'Reilly was an Irish immigrant who had a tattoo shop of his own at number 11, Chatham Square in New York City back in 1875.

In 1891, O'Reilly invented the rotary tattoo machine. His tattoo machine was the first to ever run off of electricity. It was based on the same technology that Thomas Edison used for his autographic printing pen.

The tattoo machines that are currently being used today are still based on the same technology as Samuel O'Reilly's model.

Croquet

Thanks to the Queen of Hearts playing the game of croquet in *Alice in Wonderland*, you may have always thought the game was invented in England. In fact, most people are under this assumption, as the game is very popular in England. The game is said to be a favorite of Queen Elizabeth II.

Well, despite the popularity that the game has gained in England, croquet actually wasn't invented there. Croquet actually originated from Ireland's west coast!

It's believed that the game, which rose to popularity during the 1850s, actually stemmed from a similar game that had been brought to the Emerald Isle from northwest France. There's some controversy about which French game croquet may have originated from, however. There was one game called *jeu de mail,* was similar to pall-mall or indoor billiards. One version of the game was known as *rouët* (or "wheel") was played in the lawn with multiple balls.

There was another game known as "crookey," which was similar to croquet. There are records which show that the game was played at Castlebellingham in County Louth, Ireland in 1834. It was played on the bishop's palace garden. The first record of the game being called "croquet" was during the same year. No documents provide any instruction on how the game was played, however.

The game spread like wildfire across Ireland. Records indicate that croquet got started in Ireland and migrated to Great Britain in about 1851, where it was first played on the lawn of Lord Lonsdale. It quickly spread across England, eventually leading to the All England Croquet Club, which would later go on to become Wimbledon!

Guinness

What would Ireland be without its beer? Guinness beer is, by far, one of the most well-known inventions to come out of the Emerald Isle.

It all started back in 1758 when Arthur Guinness

started brewing ales in Dublin at St. James's Gate Brewery. The following year, Guinness signed a 9,000-year lease. Yes, you read that right. *A nine-thousand-year lease.*

A decade later, Guinness exported his ale for the first time. He shipped 6.5 barrels of Guinness beer to Great Britain.

By 1778, Arthur Guinness began to sell dark beer porter. During the 1840s, Guinness's Single Stout and Double were the first beers to use the term. "Stout" was originally used in reference to a beer's strength. Eventually, the term evolved to describe the beer's body and color. "Porter" meant "plain."

Throughout the years, Guinness mostly only produced three varieties of beer: Porter or Single Stout, Double Stout or Extra Stout, and Foreign Stout.

Guinness's sales increased from 350,000 barrels in 1868 to 779,000 barrels in 1876. By 1886, the company was producing more than 1.13 million barrels a year. These increases happened even though Guinness didn't advertise or offer discounted beer.

During the Anglo-Irish Trade War in 1932, Guinness's headquarters moved to London.

Around the 1950s, Guinness changed the flavor of its ale. It began to use malted barley and roasted un-malted barley when brewing its beer. This gave Guinness its signature burnt flavor. Prior to that,

Guinness's aged brew was mixed with freshly brewed ale. This gave it a lactic acid flavor. Guinness does still have a bit of a tangy flavor, but it's unknown if this method is still used in the company's beer production process. Guinness is also known for its thick, creamy head, which it gets from mixing the beer with carbon dioxide and nitrogen when its poured.

Today, Guinness is the best-selling alcoholic beverage in Ireland and one of the most successful beer brands throughout the entire world. It's brewed in nearly 50 countries and can be found in more than 120 countries. Ten million pints of Guinness are produced in Dublin each year.

As of 2011, 850 million liters of Guinness was being sold throughout the world on a yearly basis. It might surprise you to learn that while Guinness is the best-selling beer brand in Ireland, the country does *not* sell the highest amount of Guinness throughout the world. Both Britain and Nigeria have more Guinness sales than Ireland, which ranks in at No. 3.

Although Guinness is the best-selling Irish beer, there are a few other well-known beer brands from the Emerald Isle. These include Kilkenny, Smithwick's, Murphy's Irish Stout, and Harp Lager. Kilkenny is a nitrogenated cream ale that originated from Kilkenny and is made by Guinness. Guinness also owns Smithwick's and Harp Lager.

It's not entirely a monopoly, though. Murphy's Irish Stout, which is brewed in Cork, Ireland, is owned by Heineken International.

Fun fact: Up until 2010, all Irish blood donors were offered free Guinness. The practice stopped because the country no longer wanted to promote the idea of alcohol as medicine.

RANDOM FACTS

1. The Emerald Isle is famous for Irish whiskey. It might surprise you to learn that the word "whiskey" originates from a Gaelic phrase that means "water of life." What sets it apart from other types of whiskey is that peat generally isn't used during the malting process, which gives it a smoother taste. Irish whiskey is more similar to Scotch than most other types of whiskey. At one point in time, Irish whiskey was the most popular spirit in the entire world. During the 1890s, Ireland had more than 30 distilleries. After a decline in popularity during the 19th century, however, there were only three distilleries that remained in the country. That being said, Irish whiskey has made a comeback. Sales of Irish whiskey have increased every single year since 1990. In 2017, Ireland not only had 18 Irish whiskey distilleries but there were 16 more that were about to open in the near future.

2. While Viagra was created in England, a Belfast native was a part of the team that provided research papers about the drug in 1999. Originally developed to treat angina, the drug we now know as Viagra was repurposed for an erectile dysfunction drug.

3. Cream crackers were invented by the Jacob family of Dublin, Ireland during the mid-1880s. Their invention involved allowing yeast dough to ferment for 24 hours. They later flattened it and folded it multiple times in order to create a biscuit. Today, Jacob's Cream Crackers are produced at an estimated rate of one million per hour and are sold in more than 35 countries across the world.

4. Dublin native Robert Percival, who was a college professor at Trinity College, created soda water (or sparkling water) for medicinal purposes back in 1800. Although the English Thomas Henry was actually the first to invent sparkling water, Professor Percival was an accomplished chemist who thought the carbonated water beverage would work as a cure for scurvy. J.J. Schweppe used Percival's formula, which was sold for medicinal purposes.

5. Cidona, which is a sparkling apple drink, was originally produced by the Bulmers cider brand in County Tipperary, Ireland. The apple soft drink has been around since 1955 and is a popular drink in Ireland today.

6. The bacon rasher was designed by a Waterford butcher by the name of Henry Denny. Prior to Denny's invention, the bacon curing process involved soaking large meat chunks in brine.

However, Denny experimented by using long flat pieces of meat, rather than large chunks. Instead of brine, he used dry salt. It may have seemed like a simple idea at the time, but it paved the way for the bacon industry. Denny started to export his meat to Europe and the Americas. The shelf-life and quality of the bacon were drastically improved.

7. Wi-Fi may not have been invented in Ireland, but it was founded by an Irish-Australian named John O'Sullivan. O'Sullivan was working on a CSIRO research project when he accidentally discovered Wi-Fi!

8. The modern tractor was invented in Ireland, which should come as no surprise considering agriculture leads the country's economy. Harry Ferguson was a mechanic from Growel, County Down who's credited with inventing the modern tractor. Prior to his invention, tractors and plows were separate equipment, which made it difficult and dangerous to operate them. In 1926, Ferguson became the first to combine the machinery. He used hydraulics to operate the plow. His invention not only made farming safer, but it also made it more cost effective. At 25 years old, Ferguson, who had designed his own airplane, became the first Irishman to fly a plane!

9. The armored tank was invented by Dublin native

Walter Gordon. Gordon was commissioned by Winston Churchill to build a vehicle that could withstand bullets and shrapnel and was capable of crossing trenches, flattening barbed wire, and journeying through the mud. Gordon's design changed how wars were fought. While modern armored tanks don't look anything like the original invention, the basic concept is still used to engineer the machines.

10. Milk of Magnesia was invented by James Murray from County Londonderry. Murray, who was a physician, did a lot of research on digestion. His research is what led him to create the stomach aid in 1809. Murray created the foundation of a fluid magnesia. His primary ingredient was Magnesium sulfate, which was known to relieve constipation and help with digestion. Murray named his concoction Fluid Magnesia. It was later sold as a solution that treated heartburn, indigestion, acid reflux, and gout. Murray manufactured the medicine from a factory he set up in Belfast.

11. Another one of James Murray's inventions was artificial fertilizer. He conducted trials back in 1817. Eventually, Murray developed and produced the synthetic fertilizer that we use to this day. His invention came about thanks to the Fluid Magnesia production process, which

produced potassium bicarbonate, silicate, and sodium as a byproduct. Murray had the idea to treat these chemicals with sulfuric acid, which produced what we now know as artificial fertilizer.

12. Irish soda bread is one of the country's most well-known foods, but it wasn't actually invented in the country. In Europe, the first documentation of the recipe was back in 1817 in London's "The Gentleman's Magazine." That being said, Irish soda bread has become a tradition in the country. In Ireland, soda bread is made from soft wheat or pastry flour, which gives soda bread a lower amount of gluten than regular bread flour. Soda bread varies in different areas of Ireland. Ulster is most well-known for its sweetened, wholemeal variety of soda bread, while Fermanagh is better known for its white flour soda bread. Regardless of region, one thing remains consistent: it's recommended that you mix the ingredients as little as possible and avoid kneading the bread prior to baking.

13. The safety lamp was invented by William Reid Clanny, who was born and raised in Bangor, County Down. Clanny later trained as a physician at Edinburgh and was also an assistant surgeon in the Royal Navy. Due to the 1812 Felling colliery disaster in Gateshead that caused

problems with underground lighting, there became a need for a safety lamp. Clanny designed his first safety lamp. His original design was a candle surrounded by glass. Underneath the glass, there was a trough that contained water that air was forced through. Another water chamber above allowed fumes to bubble out. Clanny won awards in 1816 and 1817 for his design.

14. The double-breasted coat was designed in Ireland. The designer of the coat was John Getty McGee, who owned a shop named McGee & Co. on High Street in Belfast. He used heavy Donegal tweed in his design, which consisted of pleats, pockets, and a belt. McGee's shop was later renamed to the Ulster Overcoat Company thanks to his design.

15. Barmbrack, which is often referred to as "brack," is a type of Irish fruitcake. The cake is filled with fruit, spices, and raisins. It's soaked in tea and whiskey overnight. It's a popular Irish snack to have with afternoon tea. For Halloween, the Irish put trinkets in the dough that are intended to give you a fortune. If you find a coin, for example, you'll come into good fortune. If you find a ring, then you'll get married within a year.

16. The Kelvin Scale was invented by William Thomson, who was born in Belfast. Thomson,

who showed signs of genius from an early age and began studying at Glasgow University at just 10 years old, came up with the lower limit to the temperature—or absolute zero—back in 1824. He invented a new temperature scale, which used zero as a starting point. After Thomson helped determined the necessary thickness of the telegraph table, he was given the title Lord Kelvin. His temperature scale was named the Kelvin Scale after him. Thomson also invented the compass that can be found on British naval ships and the reversible heat engine, which paved the way for refrigeration.

17. A boxty, or Irish potato pancake, is made from mashed potatoes and grated raw potatoes. Its origins trace back to the Irish Potato Famine days. The food was so popular in northwest Ireland that it was the inspiration of a popular folk rhyme: "Boxty on the griddle, Boxty on the pan, if you can't make a Boxty, you'll never get a man."

18. The first electric tramway in the world was invented by two brothers from County Antrim, William, and Anthony Traill. The tramway was Giant's Causeway Tramway, which spanned from Bushmills to Portrush when it first opened. Constructed in 1883, the three-foot-wide gauge line was harnessed by hydro-electric power. It

remained open until 1949, closing due to high maintenance costs and low passenger numbers. The tramway reopened two miles of its original route in 2002.

19. Irish coffee is one of the most popular recipes to come from the country. An Irish coffee is a mixture of black coffee, Irish whiskey, and sugar. It's topped off with cream. It was invented back in 1942 when a flight of American passengers was delayed in Ireland due to bad weather conditions. Joe Sheridan, who worked as the restaurant chef at the airport, put Irish whiskey in their coffee to warm them up.

20. The act of boycotting, or deliberately abstaining from buying, using or supporting certain services, businesses, organizations or people, got started in Ireland. The act was also named after an Irish native, Captain Charles Boycott. Some disgruntled people from an Irish village in Mayo came up with the concept in the late 19th century. It was during the "land war" when tenants have a difficult time gaining rights to their land. Boycott's estate imposed higher rent and threats of eviction after a poor harvest. The tenants protested against this. Instead of using violence to get what they wanted, they refused to work in his fields or stables, trade with him or do anything else they normally did to help him out.

Boycott was forced to hire new workers to harvest his crops. Eventually, Boycott ended up leaving Ireland completely.

Test Yourself – Questions

1. Chocolate milk was originally sold as:

    a. A children's drink
    b. A coffee additive
    c. A medicine

2. One of the first patients to ever have the hypodermic needle used on them to treat their pain was:

    a. Queen Elizabeth I
    b. Alfred, Lord Tennyson
    c. Florence Nightingale

3. Robert Percival invented sparkling water, believing that it could treat what?

    a. scurvy
    b. heartburn
    c. parasites

4. An Irish fruitcake is called a:

    a. Boxty
    b. Barmbrack
    c. Box cake

5. Croquet was probably based on another game, which originated from which country?

    a. France
    b. Italy
    c. Great Britain

Answers

1. c.

2. c.

3. a.

4. b.

5. a.

CHAPTER FIVE

IRELAND'S ATTRACTIONS

If you've thought about planning a trip to Ireland, then you probably know of some of the must-see attractions. But how much do you really know about them? Do you know which of Ireland's famous stones generated a phrase that's often used on St. Patrick's Day today? Do you know who's buried at Ireland's most famous church? Do you know which of Ireland's castles has been converted into a 5-star luxury hotel? Read on to find out the answers to these and other interesting facts about some of Ireland's most famous attraction.

The Phrase "Kiss Me, I'm Irish" Comes from Ireland's Famous Most Famous Stone

Have you ever wondered where the phrase "Kiss me, I'm Irish" comes from? If you guessed that its origins come from the Blarney Stone, you'd be right.

According to the legend, kissing the stone will give

you the gift of eloquence or persuasiveness. It's been said that kissing an Irish person is the next best thing.

The stone is set in a wall of Blarney Castle, which is located just outside of Cork, Ireland.

There are several legends about how the Blarney Stone got there. According to one story, the stone was brought to Ireland during the Crusades. Another legend says that the stone dates back to the 1440s when the castle's builder, Cormac Laidir MacCarthy was involved in a lawsuit and needed good luck. MacCarthy allegedly asked for help from Clíodhna, the Irish goddess of love and beauty. Clíodhna told MacCarthy to kiss the stone before he went to court. After winning the case, he installed the stone into the castle.

There's another story that says Queen Elizabeth I wanted to strip Cormac Teige McCarthy, Lord of Blarney of his land rights. Cormac wanted to change the queen's mind, but he wasn't an eloquent speaker. According to the tale, Cormac came across a woman during his travels who told him that kissing a certain stone in Blarney Castle would give him the gift of persuasive speech. Cormac, of course, kissed the stone and later was able to persuade Queen Elizabeth I to let him keep his land.

Some say the stone was actually brought to Ireland during the Crusades, while others believe it was made from the same material as Stonehenge.

Although millions of people from all over the world have kissed the Blarney Stone, it's not necessarily the easiest task. In fact, before the guard rails were installed at the castle, kissing the stone posed a risk of injury or even death. Today, one must climb the windy, narrow stairs that lead to the top of the castle. Then you must lean over backward, grabbing an iron railing, in order to get to a position to press your lips to the stone. It's done with the help of an assistant. While it is safe nowadays to kiss the Blarney Stone, it's not for people who suffer from a fear of heights.

Is kissing the Blarney Stone worth it? Winston Churchill kissed the stone back in 1912. Some believe that kissing the stone may have led him to become British prime minister in 1940 and gain his reputation as a powerful speaker.

The Blarney Stone is undoubtedly one of Ireland's biggest tourist attractions, with an estimated 400,000 people visiting the stone each year.

You Can Visit the Church Where St. Patrick Baptized People

One of Ireland's must-see attractions is St. Patrick's Cathedral. As one of Dublin's most important historic buildings, it's one of the city's most popular tourist attractions.

Located in Dublin, it's national cathedral of the Church of Ireland. This is believed to be the site where St. Patrick baptized hundreds of people to convert them to Christianity in AD 450. The church itself was built between the years of 1220 and 1260 in honor of St. Patrick. The cathedral is one of just a few buildings that remain from Dublin's medieval period.

The Lady Chapel, which dates back to 1270, has recently been restored. A new exhibition known as Lives Remembered, which features a tree sculpture and honors World War I, has also recently opened.

St. Patrick's Cathedral is the tallest and largest church in Ireland, but it's not the tallest cathedral in the country. That would be St. John's Cathedral.

Jonathan Swift, who authored *Gulliver's Travels*, served as Dean of St. Patrick's Cathedral back in the 1700s. He is one of the many people who has been buried on the site.

St. Patrick's Cathedral is well-known for its choir. The choir performs daily for most of the year.

Visitors can take a guided tour of St. Patrick's Cathedral, or use an app to self-guide themselves.

Ireland's National Parks Take Up Just 160,000 Acres of Land

Ireland is home to six national parks, which, combined, take up just 160,000 acres of land. To put this into perspective, America's smallest national park—Wrangell-St. Elias National Park in Alaska—encompasses 13.2 million acres of land.

Wicklow Mountains National Park is the largest of Ireland's six parks. Situated on 54,000 acres of land, the park is located in the Wicklow Mountains. It's a popular recreational spot for tourists.

Glenveagh National Park, which takes up approximately 41,000 acres, is located on the hillside above Glenveagh Castle. The park is mostly known for its gardens. The golden eagle was reintroduced to the park back in 2000 after being declared extinct at the local level.

Ballycroy National Park is located in the Nephin Mountains area. The park is known for its blanket bog, which is one of the largest expanses of peatland in all of Europe. It's also home to the Owenduff River, which is known for its salmon and sea trout.

Killarney National Park was the first national park to ever be formed in Ireland. It was donated to the Irish Free State by the Muckross Estate back in 1932. The park, which is set on 25,425 acres, is the only place on the Ireland mainland where you'll find red deer. It's also the most forested area left in Ireland.

Connemara National Park is located in County Galway. The park is home to blanket bog, heathland, mountains, grasslands, and forest. There's also a 19th century graveyard and megalithic court tombs that date back to more than 4,000 years.

Burren National Park—which is also known as "The Burren—is the smallest of the Irish national parks. The park takes up just 3,700 acres. It's most well-known for its temperature climate conditions and its limestones and sandstones. The park's rolling hills also contain 250 square miles of limestone pavements, which date back to when the area was beneath sea level 325 million years ago.

This Castle is Considered One of the Most Important Buildings in Ireland's History

It's one of the biggest tourist attractions in all of Dublin. But did you know that Dublin Castle is one of the most important buildings in the country's history?

The site of the castle was originally owned by a 1930s Danish Viking Fortress. During the 12th century, it was a Norman fort.

The Dublin Castle was later rebuilt by King John, the English king and first Lord of Ireland. The castle's construction was completed in the year 1230.

The castle has been the seat of government for England and Britain. In 1922, the castle was given to Ireland's newly formed Provisional Government.

Today, the Dublin Castle is where Ireland's Presidential Inauguration takes place.

For history buffs, the castle is a must-see attraction.

One of the most popular features of the castle is its gardens, which have been around since the 17th century. The castle's gardens contain three memorial gardens, including the popular garden that honors the 2003 special Olympics that were held in Ireland and the 30,000 volunteers' names that are inscribed on plaques.

Each year, the Dublin Castle hosts the Heineken Green Energy. The music festival, which takes place in May every year, attracts approximately 50,000 people to watch musicians from all over the world perform. The festival has been running since 1996. Some of the artists who have performed at the festival include Sinéad O'Connor, Beck, Van Morrison, Morrissey, Iggy Pop, Alice Cooper, Snow Patrol, the Cranberries, the Hives, the White Stripes, and more.

Kilmainham Gaol is Ireland's Most Famous Prison

If you're a historical prison enthusiast, then you won't want to miss out on Kilmainham Gaol, which is Ireland's largest and most famous unoccupied prison.

The prison is known as an icon of Ireland's dark history. Located in Kilmainham, Dublin, the prison was first built in 1796.

Children were imprisoned for things like petty theft. The youngest prisoner on record was a seven-year-old child.

The prison wasn't segregated, with men, women, and children being incarcerated, with up to five people per cell. The only lighting that was provided came from a single candle, which had to burn for two weeks at a time. Most of the prisoners spent their time in the dark and cold.

Adult prisoners were often sent to Australia.

Female prisoners, in particular, were treated very poorly. Male prisoners were given iron bedsteads, but women were forced to sleep on straw.

During the Potato Famine, Kilmainham Gaol became overwhelmed with an influx of prisoners.

It was at Kilmainham Gaol that the Irish revolution leaders of the 1916 Uprising were convicted and later executed of High Treason. The executions took place in the prison yard.

Today, Kilmainham Gaol is a museum that provides insight to the history of Irish nationalism. It's also home to an art gallery on the top floor.

The Cliffs of Moher Are One of Ireland's Most Breathtaking Views

For many, the Cliffs of Moher are what come to mind when it comes to Ireland. The breathtaking cliffs are often seen on postcards and have been featured in a few films, including *Harry Potter and the Half Blood Prince* and *The Princess Bride*. The Cliffs of Moher sees more than 1 million visitors each year, making it one of Ireland's most visited attractions.

Ireland's most famous cliffs were formed during the Carboniferous Period, which took place 320 million years ago—long before the island of Ireland even existed. Located in County Clare on Ireland's west coast, the rocky sea cliffs span across 14 kilometers and reach a maximum height of 214 meters (or 702 feet). The highest location can be found just north of O'Brien's Tower, which is a round stone tower that's located near the cliffs' midpoint. The tower was built by Sir Cornelius O'Brien back in 1835.

The word "Moher" originated from the old Irish word "Mothar," which translates to "ruined fort." Moher Fort, which now stands where a 1st century B.C. fort once stood, is the stone ruin of an old watchtower that the Cliffs of Moher are named after. Moher Tower served as a watch tower during the 1800s during the Napoleonic Wars.

You'll find a lot of seabirds at the Cliffs of Moher. In fact, it's been estimated that approximately 30,000 birds from 20 different species live in the area. Atlantic puffins can be found here. Dolphins, whales, and seals are also often sighted from the cliffs.

The view is known to be breathtaking. You can see the Aran Islands, as well as the Maumturks and Twelve Pins mountain ranges, from both the cliffs and O'Brien's Tower. You can take the Cliffs of Moher Coastal Walk, which spans 18 kilometers from Hag's Head to Doolin. You can also view the cliffs from sea level with a ferry ride.

You Can Sample Irish Beer at Guinness Storehouse

Have you ever wondered if a pint of Guinness tastes better when it's poured in Ireland? Well, you can find out for yourself during your next trip to the Emerald Isle—and not just at a local pub.

Set inside a former fermentation plant at St. James's Gate Brewery in Dublin, the Guinness Storehouse is the most popular tourist attraction in all of Ireland. As of 2017, the Guinness Storehouse was visited by 1.7 million people!

The Guinness Storehouse is a museum that surrounds a glass atrium in the shape of a pint of Guinness. The Storehouse boasts itself as the biggest pint in the world. You'll begin your tour at the bottom of the glass. You'll have a chance to see the legendary 9,000-year lease that was signed by Arthur Guinness. Then you'll travel upwards through seven floors of interactive tourists that will give you a taste of both Ireland and Guinness's brewing history.

Some of the exhibits you'll find at the Guinness Storehouse involve the brewery's founder (Arthur Guinness), ingredients, brewing, transport, cooperage, advertising, and sponsorship.

The Storehouse also offers several eateries that offer Irish cuisine. The menu includes fare with Guinness as an ingredient.

You'll top it all off with a pint of Guinness, which you can pour yourself, from the Storehouse's rooftop Gravity Bar. The best part about it all is that the pint is included in the cost of admission.

Sligo Abbey is Home to This Unique Altar

Located in northwest Ireland, Sligo Abbey is a ruined abbey that was originally built in 1253.

Sligo Abbey has quite the history. It was destroyed back in 1414 by a fire. It was later ravaged during both the Nine Years' War in 1595 and later during the Ulster Uprising in 1641.

Sligo Abbey was restored by Lord Palmerston during the 1850s.

Today, the Abbey is open to visitors.

It's home to Gothic and Renaissance tomb sculptures. Sligo Abbey is also home to the only 15th century sculptured high altar to survive in any church in all of Ireland.

Sligo Abbey is mentioned in two of W. B. Yeats' short stories: *The Curse of the Fires and of the Shadows* and *The Crucifixion of the Outcast*.

There's also a legend about Sligo Abbey. It's been said that worshippers saved the Abbey's silver bell, which was thrown into Lough Gill. Rumor has it that only those who are free from sin can hear the bell ring.

This University's Library Inspired A Famous Fictional Library

A university's library might not seem like the tourist attraction you had in mind, but if you're a fan of the *Harry Potter* series, you might want to think again.

The library from *Harry Potter and the Sorcerer's Stone* was inspired by the Long Room, the main chamber of the Old Library at Trinity College in Dublin. The Long Room is 65 meters long and is home to 200,000 books. It's widely regarded as one of the most impressive libraries in the entire world.

The library is also the permanent home to *The Book of Kells*, which is a 9th century illuminated manuscript that's often called "Ireland's national treasure." Two of the four volumes are on display at all times.

The library, which is the largest library in Ireland, isn't the only reason to visit Trinity College. It's also Ireland's oldest university. Trinity College was founded by Queen Elizabeth 1 back in 1592. Since then, a number of notable people have attended the college. Some of these include Oscar Wilde, Samuel Beckett, Jonathan Swift, and Bram Stoker.

The Rock of Cashel is Ireland's Most Visited Heritage Site

Today, the Rock of Cashel is Ireland's most visited heritage site. It's also one of the most picturesque spots in all of Ireland. Located in County Tipperary, the remarkable group of Medieval buildings is perched on a limestone rock formation in the Golden Vale. Among its buildings are the High Cross, the Romanesque Chapel, and the Hall of the Vicars Choral.

According to Irish legends, the Rock of Cashel was formed due to Devil's Bit, a mountain that's located 20 miles north. This is said to have happened when St. Patrick banished Satan to a cave, which caused the rock to land in Cashel.

Regardless of how it came to be, the Rock of Cashel was allegedly the seat of the kings of Munster for hundreds of years before the Vikings invaded the land. The King of Munster donated his fortress on the Rock of Cashel to the church in 1101.

Most of the early structures didn't survive. Today, most of the current buildings that can be found on the site date back to the 12th and 13th centuries.

The Rock of Cashel is famous for its Celtic art and medieval architecture, which is said to be the best collection in all of Europe.

In 2011, Queen Elizabeth II visited the Rock of Cashel via helicopter during her tour of the Emerald Isle.

The Aran Islands Provide an Irish Cultural Experience

Located at the mouth of Galway Bay, the Aran Islands have become a popular tourist attraction. The three islands, from large to small, are Inishmore (meaning "big island), Inishmaan (meaning "middle island"), and Inisheer (meaning "east island).

The Aran Islands are a great place to go to get a taste of true Irish culture. The Aran Islands' 12,000 inhabitants speak Gaelic as a first language. The Islanders also speak English.

Inishmore is home to the most people, with more than 800 residents living there full-time. The main town, Kilronan, is home to a number of Bed & Breakfasts.

The most popular tourist site is also found on Inishmore. Dun Aonghasa is a stone fort which encompasses 14 acres of land, dates back more than 2,500 years, and offers breathtaking views of the Ireland mainland.

Despite being the smallest island, Inisheer is home has the second highest population. It also boasts a number of sites that draw tourists, including a shipwreck, a lighthouse, and an ancient monastic site.

Dingle Bay Was the First Part of Europe Discovered by Charles Lindbergh

Dingle Bay is one of the Ireland mainland's most western points. The 25-mile bay and drains into the Atlantic Ocean. The harbor town of Dingle lays just north of Dingle Bay.

It might surprise you to learn that Dingle Bay was the first part of Europe that was discovered by American aviator Charles Lindbergh. Lindbergh took the first transatlantic flight, in which he traveled from New York to Paris. In the 1957 movie *The Spirit of St. Louis*, Lindbergh is portrayed by Jimmy Stewart. In the film, he waves to the Dingle Bay villagers as he flies over the area.

Visitors enjoy taking a boat trip on Dingle Bay to meet Fungie. Fungie is a wild bottlenose dolphin who is a favorite among tourists. The dolphin, who has allegedly lived in the bay since 1983, is said to love humans.

Fun fact: Dingle is considered to be Ireland's largest Gaelic-speaking town.

The Ring of Kerry is a Popular Scenic Route

The Ring of Kerry is a 111-mile circular tourist route in County Kerry in southwest Ireland. It's considered to be one of the most picturesque routes to take in the whole country and a must-see for tourists.

Along the way, you'll come across a number of popular stops. These include Muckross House, Staigue stone fort, and the Derrynane House, which was home to Daniel "The Liberator" O'Connell in Killarney. Ross Castle, Lough Leane, and Ladies View, which are all located within Killarney National Park, are also popular stops.

Other popular attractions during the route include Torc Waterfall, Kellegy Church, The Blue Pool, Ballymalis Castle, Ogham Stones, St. Mary's Cathedral, and Muckross Abbey—just to name a few.

During the summer, you can take a bus route. There's also The Kerry Way, a walking path that takes its own route along quieter roads. It follows much of the same route as the Ring of Kerry.

The Dublin Zoo Has a Dark History

Drawing in more than 1 million visitors a year, Dublin Zoo is one of Ireland's most popular attractions. Located in Phoenix Park, the zoo opened back in 1831.

As the largest zoo in the Emerald Isle, the zoo is

spread across 69 acres and is home to more than 400 animals. It takes part in conservation efforts for endangered species. Some of the animals it has a role in conserving include golden lion tamarins, Moluccan cockatoos, and Rodrigues fruit bats.

What you might be surprised to learn is that the Dublin Zoo has quite a dark history.

When the zoo was first opened, it was called the Zoological Gardens Dublin. The 46 mammals and 72 birds that it first opened with were donated by the London Zoo.

The founders of the zoo worked within the medical profession. While they had an interest in studying animals while they were alive, they were even more interested in studying them when they were dead. During the 1830s, people in the medical profession who weren't tied to a big medical institution had to steal cadavers from graves if they wanted to study them. Being able to obtain the cadaver of a primate meant that they no longer had to steal cadavers from graves.

In 1903, one of the zoo's most tragic events took place. One of the zookeepers was killed when he was tending to the injured foot of an elephant named Sita. Sita was put down by the Royal Irish Constabulary.

During the Easter Rising of 1916, the zoo ran out of meat. In order to save its lions and tigers, other animals from the zoo had to be sacrificed for food.

In 1989, the zoo's finances became so dire that the council considered closing it. However, the Government gave the zoo an annual grant to maintain operations.

By 2015, the Dublin Zoo saw 1.1 million visitors, making it the 3rd most popular Ireland attraction.

This Park in Dublin is Twice the Size of Central Park

Did you know that one of Dublin's parks is twice the size of Central Park in New York City? Phoenix Park in Dublin, which encompasses 1,750 acres, is the largest enclosed park in all of Europe. For comparison's sake, Central Park only takes up 843 acres. Phoenix Park is also larger than all of London's parks *combined*.

It may surprise you to learn that Phoenix Park wasn't named after the mythical bird. Its name came from the Gaelic term "Fionn Uisce," which translates to "clear water."

The park has an interesting history. It was originally started back in 1662 as a royal deer park for King Charles II. Fallow deer herds can still be found in the park to this day.

Like many other parks throughout the world, Phoenix Park was once used as a burial ground. The

Vikings once buried their dead there, making it the largest Viking cemetery outside of Scandinavia.

Ashtown Castle is the oldest building that can be found in the park. It dates back to the 1430s.

Queen Elizabeth II visited the park during her visit to Ireland in 2011 before meeting President Mary McAleese at Áras an Úachtaráin (which is basically Ireland's version of the White House).

RANDOM FACTS

1. Ashford Castle in County Galway, which dates
    back to 1228, has had a number of owners,
    including the Guinness family. Today, Ashford
    Castle is a 5-star luxury hotel that anyone can
    stay at. Since it was first constructed, it's had a
    number of famous guests including King George
    V and the future Queen Mary, John Lennon,
    Oscar Wilde, Ted Kennedy, Maureen O'Hara,
    John Wayne, Robin Williams, Brad Pitt, President
    Ronald Reagan, George Harrison, and Pierce
    Brosnan.

2. Grafton Street in Dublin is the city's most
    popular place to shop. The street is lined with
    boutiques, department stores, jewelers, and
    restaurants. It's a popular spot for buskers, so if
    you've ever wanted to see an Irish fiddler play,
    you've come to the right spot. There's also a
    statue of Mary Malone at the bottom of the street.

3. St. Stephen's Green is a city center public park in
    Dublin. Locals refer to the park as "The Green."
    With its beautiful gardens, famous Duck Pond,
    bridge, recreational area, and playground, it has
    something to offer just about everyone. During
    the 1916 Uprising, hostilities were stopped on a

daily basis so that the ducks could be properly fed.

4. Bunratty Castle & Folk Park, which is located in Shannon in County Clare, dates back to 1425. The castle was restored back in the 1950s. Today, the castle is known for its medieval banquets, but watch out. You might get sent to the castle's dungeon if you're not careful! Bunratty Folk Park is an open-air museum, with more than 30 buildings in a village setting for tourists to take in. You'll find village shops, farmhouses, streets, and the Ardcroney Church of Ireland to explore.

5. Cobh, which was once known as Queenstown, has become a tourist hotspot. Its popularity stems from the fact that it was the last port call for the Titanic before it made its maiden voyage across the Atlantic. Today, Cobh houses the only cruise terminal in the entire country. The town of Cobh is also known for St. Colman's Cathedral and the famous Deck of Cards, which is a row of colorful homes.

6. Titanic Belfast is a monument that opened back in 2012. The 130,000 square foot building provides interactive exhibits and galleries that provide visitors with the harrowing stories of the *RMS Titanic*. If you're a history buff, this is one attraction in Belfast that you won't want to miss out on.

7. Kilkenny Castle is a 12th century castle located in the heart of Kilkenny. The first wooden castle to stand in its place was built by in 1172. The Earl of Pembroke later had a stone castle rebuilt around 1202. Three of the four original towers can still be found there. Today, Kilkenny Castle and its adjoining park and grounds are open to the public today, with many events being held there.

8. The Wild Atlantic Way is a 1,553-mile tourism trail on Ireland's west coast. There are 1,000 attractions across the nine counties of Ireland that this trail will take you through.

9. The Giant's Causeway is made up of about 40,000 basalt columns, which were formed over 50 million years ago by volcanic activity. Located in Northern Ireland, the Giant's Causeway was voted the 4th greatest natural wonder in the UK.

10. Bewley's Graton Street, which used to be called Bewley's Oriental Café, in Dublin is known for its teas, coffees, and traditional Irish breakfast. It's also known for its pastries and its famous "Mary Cake," which the café has been serving up since 1940!

11. Muckross House and Gardens, which is located near Killarney in County Kerry, is a mansion that was designed in 1843 for Henry Arthur Herbert and Mary Balfour Herbert. The mansion was

once visited by Queen Victoria. The mansion and gardens are open to the public. There are also Jaunting Cars (a two-wheeled carriage that's driven by a single horse) that you can ride to view the grounds.

12. One of the most famous monastic sites in Ireland can be found Wicklow County. Glendalough, which is known as "Monastic City," was an early Christian monastic settlement that was founded in the 6th century by Saint Kelvin. The remaining buildings today mainly date back to the 10th through 12th century.

13. Newgrange is Ireland's most famous prehistoric monument. Located in County Meath, Newgrange was built in 3200 B.C., making it older than both Stonehenge and the Egyptian pyramids. The monument is a circular mound that contains an inner passageway and chambers. The coolest part about the monument is the roof box above the entrance of the passageway. During the winter solstice, the sun aligns with the roof box, filling the chamber of the passageway with light.

14. The National Museum of Ireland is a must-see for those interested in history. The museum, which is located in Dublin, is home to a number of Irish artifacts and Celtic art. Some of the things you'll find there include Irish haute couture fashion, jewelry, ceramics, furniture, and

artwork. There are exhibits devoted to Ireland's military and includes historic artifacts and uniforms. One of the permanent exhibitions focuses on Irish silver, some of which dates back to the 17th century. It's one of the best places in the country to learn more about the Emerald Isle's history.

15. The Dublin Bay Biosphere Reserve is made up of Dublin Bay, North Bull Island, and the surrounding area, which includes parts of Dublin. The biosphere provides a haven for a number of endangered species. It's also a popular spot to see many species of birds, including the waterfowl, Grey Heron, Goldeneye, Black-tailed Godwit, light-bellied Brent goose, and Red-breasted Merganser. The mountain hare can also be found in the area.

16. The Kylemore Castle was built in the 1800s as a shelter for a group of Benedictine nuns who had fled from Ypres, Belgium during World War I. Located in Connemara of County Galway, the abbey is an estate today. It's home to a beautiful Victorian garden, which is surrounded by walls. Tours and nature trail walks are offered to visitors.

17. The Hill of Tara, which is located in County Meath, is said to have once served as the ancient seat of the High Kings of Ireland. To some, it

might not seem like anything more than a grass-covered mound. However, it's home to a number of ancient monuments. There's a former church called St. Patrick's that dates back to 1822 that now serves as a visitor center where you can watch an audiovisual to understand the significance of the Hill of Tara.

18. There are a number of interesting historical burials in County Sligo. Rumor has it that Queen Maeve is buried in Knocknarea. Carrowmore is Ireland's largest Stone Age cemetery. Drumcliff is home to W. B. Yeats' grave, which is located next to the Table Mountain of Ben Bulben.

19. The Little Museum of Dublin is home to a number of permanent and temporary exhibits to help give you more insight into the lives of Dubliners. Opened in 2011, the museum is famous for its U2 exhibits, which were donated by the members of the famous Irish band. You'll also find the lectern John F. Kennedy used back in 1963 when he addressed the Irish Parliament.

20. The English Market is one of the most popular tourist attractions in Cork. The market's name is a bit ironic, considering the people of Cork like to think of themselves as being linked to Great Britain these days. Even so, the English Market is one of the area's biggest treasures. At the market, you'll find fresh seafood, quality cheeses, artisan

bread, and local produce. While the sign on Princes Street has a date of 1862, there's been a market on the grounds ever since the late 1900s. The English Market gained international fame when Queen Elizabeth II visited the market during her first trip to the Republic of Ireland back in 2011. Images of her joking with Fishmonger Pat O'Connell at the market were seen across the world.

Test Yourself – Questions

1. What is Ireland's most popular tourist attraction?

    a. St. Patrick's Cathedral
    b. The Cliffs of Moher
    c. The Guinness Storehouse

2. Phoenix Park in Dublin got its name from a Gaelic term, meaning:

    a. "Cool water"
    b. "Clear water"
    c. "Hot water"

3. Which of the following castles was once owned by the Guinness family?

    a. Dublin Castle
    b. Ashford Castle
    c. Kilkenny Castle

4. The last port call for the *RMS Titanic* was made in:

    a. Cobh
    b. Cork
    c. Belfast

5. Ireland's most famous prehistoric monument is:

    a. Newgrange
    b. The Hill of Tara
    c. Stonehenge

Answers

1. c.

2. b.

3. b.

4. a.

5. a.

CHAPTER SIX

WEIRD IRELAND: FOLKLORE, UNSOLVED MYSTERIES, AND MORE!

You already know of two of Ireland's biggest legends: the leprechaun and the Blarney Stone. But do you know of any other Irish legends and folklore? With its strong Celtic culture, there's a historic belief in magic, spirits, and monsters in the country. And that's not the only thing that's "weird" in Ireland. Do you know of some of the most haunted spots in the Emerald Isle? Have you heard of any of Ireland's most chilling unsolved mysteries? Do you know about the serial killer that may have murdered people in Leinster during the 1990s? Warning: this chapter may give you goosebumps.

The Banshee Warned Irish Families When Death Was Upon Them

The Banshee is one of the most well-known mythological creatures. Did you know that the lore started out in Ireland?

The word "Banshee" originates from the Irish word "baintsi," which translated to "fairy woman."

In Irish mythology, there are a number of ways the Banshee is described. She might present as a young, beautiful girl. Other times, she was an old woman dressed in rags. Sometimes she was a wash woman who rang out bloody clothing. Some say she wears white, has red hair, and has a ghostly complexion. In some versions of the tale, she had red eyes from crying.

There's one thing that all descriptions of the Irish Banshee have in common and that's that the woman brings an omen of death upon families who hear her scream or cry. In Leinster, her scream was said to be so piercing that it was able to shatter glass.

In many other cultures, people believe in a Banshee or Banshee-like monster. The difference is that in most cultures, it's believed that the Banshee kills its victims, whereas the Irish believe that the Banshee comes to deliver a warning to those who are already going to die. In Ireland, the Banshee is believed to be a messenger of death.

The Irish believed that there was one main Banshee who ruled over all the other Banshees. This main Banshee was known as the Ua Briaian. Her name was Aibell.

There was also a widespread belief that the Banshee would only appear to warn of death for people with authentic Irish last names, such as those beginning with "O'" (e.g. O'Brien, O'Connor) or "Mc/Mac" (e.g. McCarthy, MacLoughlin). The reason is that the Irish believed that Banshees only visited native Irish families, rather than settlers. It was believed that she was loyal to "true" Irish families and wanted to help them prepare for the loss of their loved ones.

Whether you believe in the legend of the Banshee or not, it all started out in the Emerald Isle!

The Children of Lir Was the Inspiration Behind *Swan* Lake

The Children of Lir is one of Ireland's most popular myths. It dates back to the ancient tribes of Ireland. The tale was allegedly the inspiration for the well-known ballet production *Swan Lake*.

According to the legend, Lir was the King of the Sea. Lir was married. He and his wife had four children together.

When his wife died, Lir married her sister, Aoife.

As it turned out, Aoife wasn't a loving aunt. Her first mission after getting married was getting rid of Lir's four children. So, one day, Aoife took the children to a lake and used her magical powers to transform them into swans.

There was only one way the spell could be broken: the children had to hear the sound of a Christian bell ring.

The children remained swans for 900 years. Legend has it that they spent 300 of those years on Lake Derravaragh, 300 years on Straits of Moyle, and 300 on Inishglora island.

Despite being swans, the children had their voices. The locals admired their singing.

Then, finally, during the 900th year, the children heard the sound of a Christian bell ring. In most versions of the tale, St. Patrick is the one who rang the bell that freed them of the curse, turning them back into the childhood version of themselves.

The children reunited with their father, who banished Aoife from his kingdom for what she had done.

The Mythological Giant That May Have Formed Giant's Causeway

Finn Mac Cool (or Fionn mac Cumhaill) is a mythological hunter-warrior and giant who's featured in several Irish legends.

One of the most famous legends about Finn Mac Cool involves the Giant's Causeway. According to the tale, Finn lived with his wife along the north coast in Antrim County. Finn was having an ongoing rivalry with another giant named Benandonner, who lived across the water in Scotland.

One day, Finn challenged Benandonner to a fight. Deciding that he didn't want to get his feet wet, Finn built a causeway of stepping stones to get to Scotland without putting his feet in the water. When Finn reached Scotland, he realized that Benandonner was far bigger than him and hurried back to Antrim.

When Finn returned to Ireland, he asked his wife to help him hide from Benandonner. His wife disguised him as a baby and hid him in an oversized cradle. When Benandonner arrived, he saw how big Finn's baby was and assumed that Finn himself must have been far larger. Afraid for his life, Benandonner ran back to Scotland, ripping up the Causeway's steps along the way.

Another tale says that Finn once picked up part of Ireland, which he planned to fling at his rival. It missed, however, and landed in the Irish Sea instead. This led to the formation of the Lough Neagh, a freshwater lake in Northern Ireland.

According to Irish lore, Finn is still alive to this day. The giant is believed to be sleeping inside a cave. It's said that one day he'll wake up and defend the Emerald Isle when he's needed the most. When he wakes up, he's expected to be just as strong and mighty as ever!

The Irish Beliefs Surrounding Fairies

By now, you know that the Irish had a strong belief in fairies. Leprechauns were believed to be fairies, after all. But what else do you know about traditional the Irish's belief in fairies?

The Irish's belief in fairies can be traced back to the Celtics and Pagans.

There are a number of different beliefs that the Irish held about the varying types of fairies.

For starters, it was thought that fairies lived in "fairy trees"—Hawthorn trees—or fairy forts. It was believed to be very disrespectful to tamper with these places. If you dared tamper with the fairy's home, then you could expect to be punished in the form of bad luck, sickness or even death. There were written records of these types of things happening. Even today, the government protects these sites.

It's also believed that an Irish fairy can assume any form she wants—with a human form being the most common choice. Fairies could also shift into the form of animals, as well.

Fairies in Ireland are thought to be beautiful and irresistible. They are believed to be creatures of seduction, which makes them extremely powerful. It's thought that many fairies abuse this power, however, as Irish fairies are said to bring bad luck to humans who are foolish enough to go near them.

The Pooka May Have Wreaked Havocs on Farms and Marine Towns

The Pooka—or Púca—is a mythological being the Irish once believed in. According to some versions of the tale, Pookas are a type of fairy. In other versions, they're some sort of monster.

"Púca" is an Irish word that translates to "spirit or ghost."

The Pookas are said to have dark or white fur or hair. They were believed to be shape changers, often taking on the form of a horse, goat, cat, dog or hare. This made it easy for them to destroy farms. They were believed to tear down fences and cause disturbances among the animals. They would also stand outside of farmhouses, luring innocent humans by calling their names. When the human came outside, the Pooka would carry them off into the night.

In some stories, the Pookas brought good luck to those who showed them kindness. In one story, a farmer's son named Padraig offered one of the Pookas, who had been in the form of a bull at the time, a coat. In return, the Pookas came at night to help turn the sacks of corn into flour. Padraig made the Pookas a silk suit as a gift for their work. When Padraig later got married, the Pookas left him a golden cup filled with a drink that would bring him and his wife happiness.

In other stories, the Pookas were evil and menacing. A boy who lived near Killarney said that the elders said the Pookas were once high in numbers. They described them as black, bad creatures that took the form of wild coats. Children were warned not to eat overripe blackberries, which were believed to be poisoned by the Pookas.

According to some of the legends, the Pookas were like vampires and had a thirst for blood. In other stories, they were said to eat people, who they hunted down and killed. It's believed that might have been what they did with the people who they carried away from farms.

Many stories involved Pookas causing disturbances in marine towns. They were often believed to cause interferences with the ships that were sailing away from Ireland's coast and were blamed for many shipwrecks.

Changelings Were a Popular Belief in Ireland During the 1800s

Changelings are a mythological being that many cultures have historically believed in. Legend has it that fairies, who often gave birth to deformed children, would go into the human world and swap their baby with a human baby. The babies the fairies left behind were changelings. Although changelings resembled human babies, they didn't have the same emotional characteristics. It's said that changelings are only happy when there's grief or misfortune in the home.

The Irish believed a few things about changelings that people in other countries and cultures did not. For example, the Irish believed that fairies swapped their children even with older people. They believed that new brides, expectant mothers, and beautiful people—both women and men—were most at risk.

The Irish also believed that changelings were sometimes older fairies who were brought to the human world to die.

The Irish believed that if you put a changeling in a fire, it would jump up the chimney and return the human child.

It was also thought that if you brewed eggshells, you could surprise a changeling into revealing the truth about who—and what—they really were.

According to one legend, an Irish mother with a changeling had a fairy come to her home to bring her own baby back. The fairy claimed that the other fairies had made the switch and she wanted her biological baby back.

People in Ireland strongly believed in changelings until at least 1895. This was the year when an Irish woman named Bridget Cleary was murdered by her husband. Her husband claimed that he believed that a fairy had kidnapped Bridget and left a changeling in her place. Bridget's husband burned her body either while she was alive or just after she'd died. The case was widely publicized and Cleary's husband spent 10 years in prison for manslaughter.

The Irish Myth of Dagda's Harp

According to Irish legends, the Dagda was a high priest. He had a beautiful harp, but a rival tribe stole it during a war. The tribe took the harp to an abandoned castle.

Dagda wasn't about to just let the thieves have his harp. He followed the tribe and called out to the harp, which came to him.

When Dagda struck the chords, the harp automatically played the Music of Tears, which caused everyone in the castle to cry.

The second time Dagda struck the chords, the harp began to play the Music of Mirth, leading the warriors to laughter.

The third and final time Dagda struck the chords, the harp played the Music of Sleep. This music put everyone in the castle into a deep slumber. This allowed Dagda to escape from the castle with the harp without getting caught.

Dracula May Have Been Inspired by an Irish Legend

Did you know that the story of *Dracula* was written by an Irishman? The gothic novel was written in 1897 by Bram Stoker, who was a Dublin native.

There are a number of theories on what inspired Stoker to write the famous novel. Some people the story of Count Dracula was inspired by the Romanian Vlad III Dracula (also known as Vlad the Impaler). Although, it's possible that this may have been where Stoker drew the name inspiration for Count Dracula from, historians believe the novel has nothing to do with Vlad III Dracula. Bram Stoker never went to Eastern Europe during his lifetime, and aside from his name, there are no similarities in the novels that suggest Count Dracula was inspired by Vlad the Impaler.

So, where *did* the idea come from? Most historians believe that Stoker was inspired by the Irish legend of Abhartach. Abhartach was said to be a chieftain and Irish wizard. According to the Irish lore, Abhartach was a vampire king. In Irish folklore, Dracula has the meaning of "bad blood."

Some historians also believe that Bram Stoker's mother's stories about a cholera outbreak in Sligo, Ireland during the early 1830s may have influenced *Dracula*. It's believed that he may have been inspired by the people who were buried alive during this time.

The Irish Legend of Deirdre and Naoise

The story of Deirdre and Naoise is one of the most popular legends about star-crossed lovers in Ireland.

According to the lore, Deidre was the most physically active woman in the Emerald Isle. King Conchobar, who was an elderly King, wanted her to be his wife. He asked for her hand in marriage and she said yes.

One winter's day, Deidre watched a raven flying in the sky over a calf who was being killed in the snow. Shortly after, she had a dream about a man whose "hair as black as pitch, lips as red as blood, and skin as white as snow." The man from Deirdre's dream was a warrior named Naoise, who she later went on to meet and fall in love with.

Deirdre and Naoise ran away together, but their love affair didn't last for long. King Conchobar caught word of it and vengefully killed Naoise.

Deirdre was forced to marry King Conchobar. However, her broken heart led her to commit suicide. This led her to earn the name of "Deirdre of the Sorrows."

King Conchobar was well-known for his rivalries with kings from other provinces in Ireland. According to the legend, King Conchobar ended up being killed by the petrified brain of a rival, which was fired at him from a slingshot.

The Hell Fire Club Was Dublin's Creepiest Club

Located in the Dublin Mountains, there's an old hunting lodge that's abandoned today. It was originally built as a shooting lodge back in 1725 for politician William Connolly. Connolly died before the lodge was ever completed, so he never actually lived in the lodge. Instead, it was used by the Hell Fire Club, which was made up of Lords and noblemen. They went to the lodge to take part in satanic rituals and other immoral acts.

People who have visited the lodge have claimed to have encounters with demons. The atmosphere is said to carry a sense of "evil," with some people even claiming that they can still smell brimstone.

In 2016, archaeologists discovered that the Hellfire Club was built over an ancient passage tomb. There were symbols that were carved into the dark rock that led the team to the entrance of the burial.

Researchers believe that the club's construction destroyed the ancient tomb. The tomb was a large circular mound that had a stone passageway. It's believed that lower levels of the tomb are untouched. The tomb was believed to be a part of a tomb complex that was spread across Dublin and Wicklow Counties.

Ireland's Most Haunted Castle

One could easily argue that probably just about any of Ireland's castles are haunted. That being said, the Ballygally Castle in Antrim County is considered to be one of the most haunted castles, as well as one of the most haunted places, in all of Ireland.

Why is it so haunted, you wonder? It all stems back to when one of the castle's previous owners allegedly locked his wife, Lady Isobel, inside one of the castle towers because she was unable to produce a male heir. Instead of starving to death in the tower, Lady Isobel is said to have leaped to her death on the rocks below.

Today, the castle is a hotel. Guests have claimed to see her apparition, along with the ghosts of children, roaming the castle's corridors.

Kilkenny is Said to Be Haunted

Kilkenny is said to be haunted—and for good reason. Did you know that the first witch trial in not only Ireland but the *entire world* took place in Kilkenny?

Back in 1324, Alice Kyteler was accused of witchcraft. The Bishop of Ossory attempted to have Kyteler arrested but instead ended up jailed himself due to her connections. Kyteler and her accomplices were accused of committing heresy, sacrificing to demons, making love and hate potions to corrupt Christians, murdering her past husbands, and engaging in a sexual affair with a demon, among other charges.

After being tortured, Petronella de Meath, who was one of Kyteler's servants, confessed to witchcraft.

Alice Kyteler allegedly fled from the country. It's believed that she went to England.

Petronella de Meath was flogged and burned at the stake in November of 1324.

The witch trial wasn't the only tragic thing to ever happen in Kilkenny. A great flood took place in County Kilkenny in 1763. John's Bridge collapsed when people were crossing it, leading sixteen people to drown. It has been said that both locals and tourists claim to hear scratching at the banks and see apparitions in the river below.

Ireland's "Vanishing Triangle"

Perhaps one of Ireland's most chilling unsolved mysteries is its "Vanishing Triangle."

In spite of the beauty of the Dublin Mountains, the area is home to a secret. Back in the 1990s, eight women went missing. All of the victims were in their late teens to forty years of age. All of the disappearances took place in a geographical area that the media began referring to as the "Vanishing Triangle." The "triangle" roughly borders Leinster.

The theory was that the women were murdered by a serial killer, who likely disposed of their bodies in the mountains.

The disappearances began in 1993 when an American student named Annie McCarrick went missing. The 26-year-old was last seen at Johnnie Fox's Pub in Glencullen in March of that year.

The last woman to go missing was Deidre Jacob in July of 1998. The 18-year-old was home from college at St. Mary's. Jacob had been running errands in Newbridge town and then went back to her family's home. She was last spotted in the afternoon just yards away from their house.

Although the disappearances stopped in 2000, interest in the case restarted in 2012 when a 30-year-old pregnant woman named Aoife Phelan went missing when she was walking home from a friend's house. Phelan's remains were later found and a 24-year-old man was charged with her murder. He was too young to have any connection with the other disappearances.

A man named Larry Murphy, who had been found guilty of rape and attempted murder of a woman in the Wicklow Mountains in 2001, was considered a suspect. He was interviewed about the disappearances of Jacob, McCarrick, and Jo Jo Dollard, who disappeared in 1995 when she hitch-hiked at the age of 21.

Although no charges have even been brought against Larry Murphy due to lack of evidence, Murphy had connections to at least one of the victims. He had done carpentry work owned by Deidre Jacob's grandmother. In an interview on the *Ray Darcy Show*, however, Jacob's mother said that she believed she knew who had killed her daughter and that it wasn't Murphy. Some find it suspicious that no other disappearances occurred throughout most of the 2000s, while Murphy was in prison for unrelated crimes. Others believe this is merely a coincidence.

Even though the Gardai (or Irish police) receive regular tips, no charges have been made in connection with any of the disappearances. None of the "Vanishing Triangle" victims' remains have been found to this day.

The Disappearance of Mary Boyle

For most families in Ireland, St. Patrick's Day is a reason to celebrate. This can't be said for Mary Boyle's family, however. In 1977, Mary Boyle, who was six years old at the time, disappeared.

Mary Boyle and her family were visiting her grandparents' home in Ballyshannon, County Donegal.

That afternoon, Mary followed her uncle to visit neighbors who lived about 500 yards away from her grandparents' house. Halfway across the marshy field that led to the neighbors' house, Mary turned around and headed back in the direction of her grandparents' home. That was the last time she was ever seen.

A few people were questioned and considered suspects early on, but no charges were ever made. Robert Black, who was later convicted of killing four girls between the years of 1981 and 1986, was a cross-border truck driver who may have been in the area at the time of Boyle's disappearance. Black's van was identified outside a pub in Annagry in County Donegal around the time of Boyle's disappearance and a witness claimed they heard crying and whimpering from the back of the van. Black hasn't been charged.

Mary's twin sister, Ann, believes that her twin was murdered by someone she knew. Ann has claimed that someone close to her has told her who killed her sister, but neither the source of information nor the killer has ever been arrested.

It's also believed that political interventions may have prevented suspects from being charged in the Boyle's disappearance.

Mary Boyle is Ireland's longest missing person to date.

The Legend of the Selkie

Have you ever heard of a "Selkie"? The mythological creature is Ireland's version of a mermaid.

The Irish did believe in mermaids, which were sometimes referred to as "merrow." However, they also believed in something that's known throughout the world as a Selkie.

The Selkie is said to very similar to a mermaid, except for one difference: they were shapeshifters. During the nighttime hours, Selkies looked like humans. During the daytime, however, they took the form of brown seals.

Selkies were said to be very beautiful when they were in their human form. They were all said to have brown eyes. They were also believed to be nude during the nighttime hours, which was one of the ways to know if it was a human or a Selkie. According to some of the legends, sailors who were able to catch a Selkie at night married them. For the rest of the Selkie's life, she would serve as a patient wife who would help her sailor husband navigate the sea.

It was said that the seal wife sometimes left her sailor husband/captor to rejoin her seal husband. In some versions of the legend, the only way the Selkie could return to the sea would be if her captor released her. But even if she *did* go back to the sea, she would continue to guard human families while she was on both sea and land.

Selkies aren't the only time seals appear in Irish mythology. It was also believed that the Conneely family of Connemara descended from seals. It was considered taboo for the Conneely family (many of which later changed their last name to Connelly) to hunt for seals. In fact, it was believed that hunting seals would bring bad luck to them.

RANDOM FACTS

1. Niall of the Nine Hostages was believed to be a mythical Irish high King, who regained between the years of 379 and 405. It was said that Niall had the most children in history. It turns out, however, that there may be some truth to this Irish legend. Professor Dan Bradley at Trinity College's research has found that 3 million men all descended from one Irish man, who may have been Niall. It's thought that 1 in 12 Irish men and 1 out of 50 New Yorkers may have descended from Niall. Since Irish surnames come from one's parental line, it's thought that this may be why the surname "O'Neill" (which means "son of Niall") is so common around the world.

2. There are a number of myths surrounding Phoenix Park in Dublin, but one of the creepiest is the Phoenix Man. The Phoenix Man has been described a couple of ways. Some claim that he's young and thin. Others say that he's a heavyset middle-aged man. Regardless of which form the Phoenix Man takes, one thing remains consistent: people who walk through Phoenix Park when night falls hear low moans and grunts . The sounds come from the wooded areas surrounding the

park. You'll know the Phoenix Man is nearby when you hear the sound of the bushes shaking! It's even been said that there's more than one Phoenix Man.

3. Ancient excarnation—which is when bodies are allowed to decompose in one area and later buried somewhere else—took place at Knocknarea Cave. Back in 2014, a team of archaeologists uncovered small amounts of bones and skeletal fragments that belonged to a man who died approximately 5,500 years ago and a child who died about 5,200 years ago. Archaeologist Dr. Marion Dowd said that the small amounts of bone fragments found, suggest that the bodies were later buried somewhere else. While it's likely that the bodies were buried somewhere nearby, it's still unknown where. Knocknarea is County Sligo's highest mountain and contains Queen Maeve's cairn, which is a pile of stones used as a memorial or headstone marker.

4. Cúchulainn is believed to be an ancient Celtic hero warrior. He is believed to have superhero-like strength. He's thought to be super-fast and able to outrun anyone. The Celts also believed that he was able to both throw and catch a javelin, spear, and ball at the same time. County Louth is often referred to as "Cúchulainn country" because the majority of legends about Cúchulainn are said to

have happened in the region, where the hero-warrior is believed to have grown up.

5. Balor was said to be a giant who possessed a single poisonous eye on his forehead. When he opened his eye, it released fire. Lured from where he lived on Tory Island, Donegal, the giant was said to have been blinded in a battle and accidentally burned his own army to the ground. According to local lore, this caused a hole to be seared into the ground, which was later filled with water, forming Sligo's Lough na Suil (the Lake of the Eye). The lake is said to drain and then later refill itself every few hundred years—or more recently, every 20 years or less.

6. The Tuatha Dé Danann, which was also known as the "tribe of the gods," were mythical rulers of Ireland. It was said that the tribe of the gods came to earth on black clouds and landed on the mountains in Connaught. There were four talismans that the tribe was believed to rule over Ireland with: The Sword of Light, the Spear of Lugh, the Cauldron of Dagda, and the Stone of Fal. When they were eventually defeated in battle, the tribe of the gods went to the Underworld where they served as the keepers of the fairies. The legacy of the Tuatha Dé Danann still lives on even to this day. Remember the goddess Éire that Ireland got its name from? Éire was believed to be

a part of the tribe of the gods.

7. There's an old Irish legend about Loftus Hall in County Wexford. Charles Tottenham, his second wife, and his daughter Anne were taking care of the mansion in 1666 while the Loftus family were away. One stormy night, a ship arrived at Hook Peninsula, which is where the mansion is located. A young man was invited inside the mansion. He quickly grew very close with Anne. One night, the family and the stranger were playing cards. Anne bent over to pick up a card and noticed that the stranger had cloven feet. In some versions of the tale, they were covered in blood. When Anne questioned the man about his feet, he went up through the roof. According to some versions of the story, he announced that he was the Devil first. The man left a large hole in the ceiling. Not long after, Anne allegedly became mentally ill. It has been said that family was so embarrassed by Anne's behavior that they locked her away in the Tapestry Room until she died there in 1975. Rumor has it that the hole was never able to be properly repaired. It's said that, even to this day, a part of the ceiling in the Card room is different from the rest of Loftus Hall. Some believe that the cloven-hoofed stranger came back to the house and continues to haunt it to this day, even after multiple attempts at exorcisms.

8. The White Lady is said to wander the grounds at

Charles Fort in Cork. The apparition, which is frequently seen, is said to be that of the daughter of the fort's commander. When the young woman's father shot the man who she was engaged to be married to, she threw herself in the ocean. Today, the woman's apparition wears a wedding dress as she walks the grounds at Charles Fort.

9. Renovations that took place at St. Columb's Cathedral back in 1867 allegedly disturbed the grave of former bishop William Higgins. After Higgins' grave was moved inside the cathedral, things began to get... well, strange. Workers started to report a number of odd occurrences, such as the sound of unexplained footsteps, the organ playing entirely on its own, and apparitions that began to appear in photographs.

10. It has been said that the spirit of a murdered jester has been seen wandering the grounds at Malahide Castle. Rumor has it that the jester, whose name was Puck, fell in love with Lady Elenora Fitzgerald, who was being kept prisoner at Malahide Castle. Puck was allegedly stabbed in the heart. Puck allegedly claimed he was going to haunt the castle once he was dead. Locals believe that he stayed true to his word.

11. Leap Castle is thought to be one of the most haunted castles in all of Ireland. Perhaps one of

the most haunting stories is how the Bloody Chapel earned its name. Back in 1250, two brothers were competing for the family seat. One of the brothers was a priest, who was giving mass in the chapel of the castle when his brother plunged a sword into his heart. Skeletons have also been discovered at the castle.

12. When there's blood on the pavements, Irish lore says that the Demon Drink might have been responsible. The demon, who is said to resemble an elf, is believed to be able to possess both men and women at night. It's said that the Demon Drink can cause even the nicest people to turn evil. People allegedly wake up the following day with no memory of being a part of a near-fatal assault the night before. The worst part about it all is that the Demon Drink is believed to live in every town in Ireland, meaning no one is safe when they go outside at night.

13. The case of Joseph Michael Maloney and Michael O'Shea is one of the most mind-boggling cases to ever take place in Ireland. Joseph Michael Maloney was a resident of Rochester, New York in 1967 when he allegedly slipped methyl alcohol into his wife's drink at their son's 5th birthday party. His wife, June, died nine days later. Maloney was the main suspect and was arrested and charged with murder. Maloney requested to

be committed for psychiatric evaluation at Rochester State Mental Home. He was committed but because he had been a former employee, he knew the layout of the hospital well enough to easily escape. Things got strange in 1973, however, when the Dublin gardai made a routine call about a burglary at the home of Michael O'Shea. When the police took fingerprints at the crime scene, they needed O'Shea's fingerprints to exclude them from evidence. They were shocked to find that O'Shea's fingerprints matched Joseph Maloney's. Since there was no extradition agreement between the United States and Ireland at that point in time, Michael O'Shea couldn't immediately be held for the New York murder— not immediately, at least. The Irish police moved slowly until the extradition agreement went into effect in 1985. While he was held in prison, a legal technicality allowed for O'Shea's extradition to the United States be overturned by the Irish Supreme Court. O'Shea was released from prison in June of 1986. Throughout the entire process, O'Shea always denied that he was Joseph Michael Mahoney. After his release from prison, O'Shea was never seen or heard from again.

14. Most of the schools in Ireland have been blessed

by a Bishop and are named after a Saint. Rumor has it that children who have never been baptized are educated with children whose parents identify as Atheists. Known as "Limbo Schools," these schools are believed to be located far away from developed areas. Students who attend these schools are not given any religious teachings. According to local lore, students who go to these schools are cursed and forced to constantly smile.

15. The Black Cat of Killakee is a black cat that's believed to have been roaming the halls and grounds of the Killakee House in Dublin for hundreds of years. The legend drew a lot of attention back in 1968 when a couple bought the then-rundown house, which they planned to renovate. The workers began to report a number of strange events at the house. They claimed that an oversized black cat with demon eyes was haunting them. The cat would appear and then vanish, terrifying the workers. At first, the woman who owned the house thought that the workers were only being superstitious. Not long after, however, she and her husband began to witness the same thing. The black cat would also appear in the house's hallways—even when the doors were closed and locked—and snarl at people to scare them away. The cat frightened

the couple so much that they had an exorcism performed at the house. For a few months, there were no signs of the cat. However, a séance that was held on the house's grounds allegedly brought the cat back—along with the spirits of two nuns.

16. The Brazen Head is Dublin's oldest pub, so it might not surprise you to learn that it has a history of allegedly being haunted. One of the pub's former customers, who was named Robert "Bold" Emmet, was hanged back in September of 1803. Since then, there have been reports of Bold's apparition sitting at the bar. It's said that Bold is on the lookout for his executioner, who was another of the pub's most frequent patrons.

17. It should come as no surprise that Kilmainham Gaol is one of the most haunted spots in Dublin. There have been reports of apparitions walking in the old prison yard, where numerous executions took place. In the 1960s, workmen who restored the old prison reported a number of unusual occurrences, such as lights flicking on and off and footsteps in the deserted corridors when no one was there. The workers even reported gusts of wind that were so strong they were knocked over!

18. Saint Michan's Church in Dublin is said to be haunted. On the outside, it looks like nothing

more than an average church. It's what's hidden under the church in the cellar that will give you goosebumps. The coffins in the cellar are said to contain bones, skulls, and human remains. There are even four mummies down there with open caskets for viewing.

19. It's believed that there are monsters that lurk in Ireland's waters. Known as the Dobhar Chu, the monsters are said to be "water hounds" that have a craving for human flesh. The monster is believed to be approximately seven feet long or about the size of a crocodile and resembles both an otter and a dog. The Dobhar Chu is said to be very fast in both the water and on land and also makes a loud, chilling screeching noise. One of the earliest accounts of the monster allegedly took place back in September of 1722 when a woman named Grainne Ni Conalai was washing her clothes at Glenade Lake in County Leitrim. Her husband allegedly heard her screaming, but when he got there, it was already too late. The Dobhar Chu had already killed her. Grainne's husband stabbed the monster in its heart, but its shrieks only woke up another monster who tried to go after him. The man managed to kill the second monster. Grainne's headstone is located in Conwal Cemetery in Glendale and mentions the beast that allegedly killed her. Since then,

there have been numerous reports of the Dobhar Chu throughout Ireland's waters. The most recent sighting was in 2003 when a couple allegedly saw one of the monsters off Omey Island in Connemara.

20. In September of 1884, the *HMS Wasp* was sent to the island of Inishtrahull off Donegal. Its mission was to evict three poor families that resided there. The ship never reached its destination, however. Instead, it ended up hitting the rocks below Tory Lighthouse. How did the ship crash? No one knows for sure. It may have just been a tragic accident, but some believe that dark forces may have played a role. Rumor has it that the Islanders had put a curse on the ship to prevent anyone from being evicted.

Test Yourself – Questions

1. What Irish myth was *Dracula* probably based on?

   a. Abhartach
   b. Pooka
   c. Dobhar Chu

2. The Irish believed that Banshees:

   a. Killed Irish people who heard her screams
   b. Warned people of death
   c. Warned true Irish people of death

3. The first witch trial in the entire world took place in which Irish town/city?

   a. Dublin
   b. Kilkenny
   c. Belfast

4. An Irish variation of a mermaid is a:

   a. Pooka
   b. Selkie
   c. Dobhar Chu

5. The Devil is believed to have played cards before leaving a hole in the ceiling at which of Ireland's mansions?

   a. Loftus Hall
   b. Powerscourt Estate
   c. Farmleigh

Answers

1. a.

2. c.

3. b.

4. a.

5. a.

DON'T FORGET YOUR
FREE BOOKS

GET THEM FOR FREE ON
WWW.TRIVIABILL.COM

MORE BOOKS BY BILL O'NEILL

I hope you enjoyed this book and learned something new. Please feel free to check out some of my previous books on Amazon.

Made in the USA
Monee, IL
29 April 2023

32676817R00098